SPORTS CAR COLOR HISTORY

CORVETTE STING RAY
1963–1967

Mike Mueller

Motorbooks International
Publishers & Wholesalers

First published in 1994 by Motorbooks International Publishers & Wholesalers, PO Box 2, 729 Prospect Avenue, Osceola, WI 54020 USA

The information in this book is true and complete to the best of our knowledge. All recommendations are made without any guarantee on the part of the author or Publisher, who also disclaim any liability incurred in connection with the use of this data or specific details

We recognize that some words, model names and designations, for example, mentioned herein are the property of the trademark holder. We use them for identification purposes only. This is not an official publication

Motorbooks International books are also available at discounts in bulk quantity for industrial or sales-promotional use. For details write to Special Sales Manager at the Publisher's address

Library of Congress Cataloging-in-Publication Data Available

ISBN 0-87938-788-2

On the front cover: This handsome 1965 L79 coupe belongs to Al and Sharon Koeberlein of White Heath, Illinois.
On the frontispiece: Chevrolet Public Relations
On the title page: The rare and brutal 1967 L88 Corvette. Only twenty of these 427-powered beasts were built. This one is owned by Roger and Dave Judski of Roger's Corvette Center in Maitland, Florida.
On the back cover: With a 435hp 427 under the hood, motivation is never an issue for this very desirable 1967 L71 Sting Ray. Chet and Deb Miltenberger of Winter Park, Florida, own this example.
Back cover inset: A very early 1965 396 Corvette. *Chevrolet Public Relations*

Printed and bound in Hong Kong

Contents

Acknowledgments

I've been a sucker for Sting Rays for as long as I can remember, even before the days when I first started making high-performance noises with my lips. Funny thing, I can't recall much of anything before the first grade, but I can still see that new 1963 Corvette like it was yesterday—and I was barely four years old when Larry Shinoda's stunning split-window coupe first hit the streets. Even then I must've had my priorities in order.

In any case, some thirty years and many, many pounds later I now find myself writing all about the cars I've loved—albeit from afar—for so long. Or not so long considering your perspective. Not only that, but I've also been allowed to burn a few rolls of film on these lovely creations, a task that hands down represented much more pleasure than work. From any angle, these fiberglass two-seaters can be almost hypnotizing, a fact I'd filed away into the back of my Pabst-clouded brain only to rediscover it with only one look through my Hasselblad's viewfinder. Timeless? Classic? Sex on wheels? Decide for yourself,—I've obviously already made up my mind.

If anything, the first-generation Sting Ray's ability to continue turning heads for five years with that same curvaceous body ought to be proof enough of this machine's claim to the gearhead's hall of fame. Most mere mortal automobiles become old news almost as soon as they hit the street, and the average American car buyer is certainly no stranger to the "what-have-you-done-for-me-lately" attitude. What did Zora Duntov and Bill Mitchell do for Corvette buyers in 1963?

First and foremost, they gave them a ride to the top of the world. Chevrolet's cute little two-seater had already salted away undeniable honors as this country's only sports car in the late 1950s—"only" was easy enough, it was the "sports car" part that the Corvette had to earn. As for "this country's," with the Sting Ray in 1963 came the chance to extend those boundaries. Sure, Jaguars, Ferraris, and Aston-Martins were superior sports cars, but they were also priced much higher and weren't inhibited by the ebb and flow of Detroit's mass-market agenda.

That Duntov managed to slip independent rear suspension under his baby was achievement enough considering the dreaded retooling-cost hurdle ever-present at every turn in Detroit. Pushing the envelope out even further by adding standard four-wheel discs in 1965 only helped reaffirm the legend of both man and machine. In its supreme form, the so-called "midyear" Corvette was a sports car that

The author with his first Corvette, circa 1961. He's still looking for his second. Nancy Mueller photo

could go, stop, turn, and travel. And it could also haul, survive everyday traffic, and live long enough to see most of its foreign rivals become museum pieces—and all this for only a couple hundred bucks, plus four grand.

Of course Zora Duntov was always looking well ahead of what reality could stand, and that's the only reason you can possibly mention "disappointed" and "Duntov" in the same sentence when talking about the Sting Ray. Zora always wanted a supreme mid-engine sports car,

a perfectly balanced world-beater that General Motors would never build in a million years. Looking at the car GM could build, Duntov wasn't quite happy with its weight, and there was very little he could do about its nasty habit to lift at high speeds. And adding a heavy big-block V-8 in 1965 wasn't exactly the direction he wanted to go, but it was the way peer pressure was directing the Corvette.

So what if Duntov's ideals were a bit high-minded? As so often is the case, shooting for the sky only helps raise the sights of all around you, while asking for far too much many times leaves you with more than you deserved. All this analogous mumbo-jumbo aside, the distance

between Duntov's ideals and GM's production realities wasn't that much greater than the gap between the common Corvette's ultimate abilities and the expectations of most average buyers. Translation: Duntov may have wanted more than he ended up with, but what he ended up with was more than enough to thrill the typical Yankee. And it still is, or at least it is from this typical Yankee's point of view.

The first-generation Sting Rays were finally winding down their five-year run when *Car Life* magazine paid tribute to Chevrolet's fiberglass legacy late in 1967. As *Car Life's* John Tomerlin saw it, the Sting Ray had emerged to fill needs that were uniquely American. "What was needed was an agile, responsive car, yet one that would be comfortable on long trips," he wrote. "What was needed was a high-performance, safe cornering, safe stopping car, yet one that any garage mechanic could service. What was needed was a car small enough to be road sensitive, powerful enough to blow off the (rolling living room,) yet one that could be equipped with air conditioning, stereo tape deck and automatic transmission." No finicky E-type Jaguar with its cramped quarters, limited conveniences, and temperamental mechanicals would do, no sir. "What was needed," Tomerlin concluded, "was the Corvette."

As usual, putting together my tribute to the midyear Corvettes required much help from many people, all who deserve far more than the humble thanks I'm preparing to dish out here. First, I must take time to thank Donald Farr, editorial director at Dobbs Publishing Group in Lakeland, Florida. Donald somehow saw fit to give me my start in this business, and has continued to bend over backward to offer assistance whenever I've asked. Allowing me to use Dobbs' library for my initial research was instrumental to kicking this project off the ground. A tip of the hat also goes to DPG's Paul Zazarine and Greg Pernula, editor and managing editor, respectively, of *Corvette Fever*. Both never failed to pick up the other end of the phone line when I had a question and graciously allowed me to ransack *Corvette Fever*'s files.

Noted author and Corvette restoration expert Noland Adams also went well beyond the call of duty once I came pleading. National Corvette Restorers Society official Bill Locke down in West Palm Beach, Florida, was a great help as well. Spending a few hours with former Chevrolet engineer and fellow Floridian Bob Clift was both educational and enter-taining, as has been my time with racing engine builder and Corvette collector Bill Tower of Plant City, Florida. Well-travelled Corvette enthusiast Ray Quinlan, of Champaign, Illinois, chipped in with his usual enthusiasm and helped locate various photogenic feature subjects.

Photographic support was also supplied by Melissa Garman at Chevrolet Public Relations, and I can't forget Lynn Cordaro, of Chevrolet's press fleet in Atlanta, who actually gave me the keys to a 1993 40th anniversary convertible, which I then promptly photographed with a 1963 split-window coupe owned by Ed and Diann Kuziel of Tampa. Roger and Dave Judski, of Roger's Corvette Center in Maitland, Florida, along with Roger's right-hand man Jeff Harris, have been incredibly cooperative as well. Way to use your head, Dave.

Valuable historical photos also came from diehard Chevy fan Pat Chappell, Jonathan Mauk at the Daytona International Speedway archives, veteran racing photographer Dave Friedman, and Joy Laschober of Bob Bondurant's School of High Performance Driving in Chandler, Arizona. At the bottom of the pile was my good friend and ever-present photographic technician, Rob Reaser, who will never cease to amaze me with his all-American work ethic.

As for obligatory credits, there's my brother Dave Mueller, of Flatville, Illinois. It was Dave's able-bodied support during countless photo shoots in the Midwest heat last summer that undoubtedly allowed me to make it home alive. And speaking of those trips, they would've never been possible if my parents, Jim and Nancy Mueller, hadn't allowed me back into the old homestead in Champaign, Illinois, for a week here and a month there while I burned up the interstates in search of midyear Corvettes. Fi-nally, there's my brother-in-law, Illinois State Trooper Frank Young, who kept my nights jumping during those trips with more Yahtzee than one human being could possibly stand. Frank, may the dice be with you.

Most importantly, laurel and hardy handshakes are extended to all the Corvette owners who allowed their two-seaters to be photographed for this book. In general order of appearance, they are:

1961 Corvette, Elmer and Sharon Lash, Champaign, Illinois; 1962 Corvette, Ed and Diann Kuziel, Tampa, Florida; 1963 coupe, Ed and Diann Kuziel, Tampa, Florida; 1963 convertible, Roger and Dave Judski, Roger's Corvette Center, Maitland, Florida; 1963 Z06 coupe (silver), Bob Lojewski, Cook County, Illinois; 1963 vintage racing coupe, Ron Lowenthal, Davie, Florida; 1963 Grand Sport coupe #005, Bill Tower, Plant City, Florida; 1964 coupe (Saddle Tan), Howard and Ginny Coombs, Sanford, Florida; 1964 fuel-injected convertible, Al and Sharon Koeberlein, White Heath, Illinois; 1964 XP-819 rear-engined prototype, Marvin Friedman, Hallandale, Florida; 1965 396 convertible, Lukason and Son Collection, Florida; 1965 L79 coupe (maroon), Al and Sharon Koeberlein, White Heath, Illinois; 1965 fuel-injected coupe (maroon), Gary and Carol Licko, Miami, Florida; 1966 convertible (red), Ed and Diann Kuziel, Tampa, Florida; 1966 coupe, Bob and Linda Ogle, Champaign, Illinois; 1966 427 convertible, Sam Pierce, Anderson, Indiana; 1967 427 convertible (yellow), Bernie Siegel, Lakeland, Florida; 1967 L71 427 convertible, Chet and Deb Miltenberger, Winter Park, Florida; 1967 coupe, Ed Augustine, Clermont, Florida; 1967 L88 coupe, Roger and Dave Judski, Roger's Corvette Center, Maitland, Florida.

Thanks so much everyone.

Chapter One

1953–1962
Sting Ray Roots

F orty years old and still running strong. Proving that "middle-aged" doesn't always mean on the downhill slide, Chevrolet's Corvette still stands tall today—four decades after its humble birth—as America's preeminent sports car. Rivals, copies, impostors, they've all come and gone, from Kaiser-Darrin, to Cobra, to Viper. While Detroit's latest attempt to unseat the King of the Hill does have an advantage as far as sheer brute force is concerned, Dodge's Viper roadster can't match General Motors fantastic plastic two-seater in class, comfort, and convenience, not to mention tradition. Regardless of Chrysler Corporation's claims, a rich reputation of performance and prestige like this doesn't come about overnight.

And to think Chevrolet's top brass nearly gave up on their fiberglass roadster after only about eighteen months on the road. Offered solely in Polo White with a red interior and six-cylinder power, the first Corvette rolled off a makeshift production line in Flint, Michigan, on June 30, 1953. A tad more than forty years to the day later, car number one million—appropriately painted Arctic White with red upholstery—emerged from the Corvette plant in Bowling Green, Kentucky, on July 2, 1993, proving that at least someone at GM believed in the idea. Zora Arkus-Duntov perhaps?

Despite the Corvette faithfuls' reverent references to Duntov as the father of their fiberglass fantasies, he wasn't even a member of the family at the Corvette's time of birth. When Duntov joined Chevrolet Motor Division's research and development team in May 1953, the original Corvette form was already cast and would roll-on basically unchanged—save for the addition of V-8 power in 1955—through three model runs. Duntov's contributions didn't really kick in until the redesigned Corvette debuted in 1956.

An intriguing, innovative attraction, Chevrolet's initial Corvette turned quite a few heads early on, then quickly fell from grace. After 300 Polo White roadsters were built from June to December 1953, planners boldly projected sales of 10,000 second-year models. Actual production for 1954 reached only 3,640, however, with about one-third of the total sitting unsold at year's end, seemingly proving to many at GM that it was time to carefully consider the Corvette's fate. Although sales sunk to a mere 700 in 1955, not everyone was ready to give up and go home. It was Duntov's determined direction that helped turn things around, as Corvette production increased every year through 1966. Most notable among the

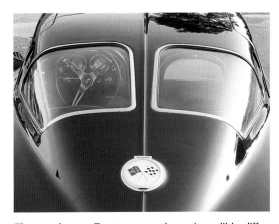

Then and now. Ten years made an incredible difference as far in the development of America's only sports car—comparing Chevrolet's first Corvette in 1953 with the stunning 1963 Sting Ray was simply no contest. Thirty years later, the Corvette tradition is still running strong, a fact commemorated by Chevrolet in the form of a special 40th anniversary model offered as both a convertible and coupe in 1993.

many feathers placed in Duntov's engineering cap during the Corvette's early development were the fabled "Duntov cam" and Ramjet fuel injection, unveiled in 1956 and 1957, respectively.

Duntov's Roots

Born in Belgium to Russian parents on Christmas Day, 1909, Zora Arkus-Duntov took an interest in mechanics while a teenager living in Russia. By age thirteen he was fascinated by motorcycles; at fourteen, he was at work designing a motor-driven "ice sled." After entering the uni-

Chevrolet chief engineer Ed Cole (left) and division chief Tom Keating examine Harley Earl's Corvette show car at GM's Motorama auto show, held in January 1953 at New York's Waldorf-Astoria hotel. It was Cole's enthusiastic support of Earl's sporting ideal that helped transform the Corvette from dream car to production reality. Having joined Chevrolet as its top engineer in April 1952, Cole later rose to the division's general manager chair in July 1956.

versity at Leningrad in 1924, Duntov followed his parents three years later to Germany where he studied at Darmstadt and Berlin. His graduation thesis paper on supercharging was published in Berlin in 1934, leading to a job designing supercharger compressors soon used on various European sports cars. From there, Duntov took a position with Mondiale in Belgium, where he penned a machine-tool lathe design. Next came work designing diesel engines for a locomotive manufacturer in Paris, during which time he continued toying with sports cars and took up race driving, a growing passion that was temporarily shelved with the coming of World War II.

Duntov joined a French bomber crew in 1939, but was grounded once Vichy France, allied with its German occupiers. Then, as part of a US plan to rob the Axis powers of as many valuable professional minds as possible, Duntov, along with about 5,000 other Europeans, was given an American visa and an invitation to

leave France for the United States, which he and his family did in December 1940. After working a short time as a consulting engineer, Zora joined forces with brother Yuri in 1942 and opened a small machine shop in New York, an outfit that eventually became the Ardun Mechanical Corporation, Ardun being short for *Arkus-Duntov*. War-time projects included various aviation components, but more to Zora's liking was a postwar contract with Ford Motor Company.

In 1947, Dearborn designers turned to the Ardun company looking for help in making Ford's venerable, somewhat underpowered "flathead" V-8 more suitable for heavy-duty truck applications. Duntov's solution was an overhead-valve conversion kit featuring aluminum cylinder heads with hemispherical combustion chambers, centrally located spark plugs, and inclined valves. Although the legendary Ardun heads did boost the flathead V-8's power, by the time they were ready for market in 1949 Ford had decid-

The first regular-production Corvette is shown here rolling of the makeshift assembly line in Flint, Michigan, on June 30, 1953. Note the plain Bel Air wheel covers. Exclusive Corvette covers were not ready in time for production leaving Chevrolet no choice but to equip the early models

with passenger car wheel covers. Although is not known exactly how many 1953 Corvettes left the line with Bel Air wheel covers, best guesses put the number at around twenty-five. Total 1953 Corvette production was 300.

Although Zora Arkus-Duntov has long been hailed as the "father of the Corvette," it was Harley Earl who actually deserves the credit for the Corvette's creation. Earl, whose tenure as head GM stylist began in 1927, started toying with the idea of a small, sporty two-seater in 1951. A plaster model was constructed in 1952, followed by a Motorama show car in 1953. Corvette production commenced at the end of 1953 on a makeshift assembly line in Flint, Michigan. Earl retired as GM Styling's top man in December 1958, passing the baton to his hand-picked successor, Bill Mitchell.

ed to use its own enlarged Lincoln V-8 for its truck fleet. Duntov's innovative ohv conversion kits were left to find homes in various race cars, some of which were still tearing up American drag strips into the early 1960s.

Perhaps most prominent among Ardun head fans was Britain's Sydney Allard, who, in 1949, began offering Duntov's ohv Ford flathead conversion in his J2 Anglo-American sports racer hybrids. Soon afterward, Duntov sold his New York firm and went to work in England for Allard, both as an engineer and a race driver. Two years later, despite a campaign among the British automotive press to "keep Duntov," he returned to the United States, taking a job with Fairchild Aviation in Long Island, New York, in the fall of 1952. Before leaving England he had written Chevrolet chief engineer Ed Cole, hinting at his interest in a job, but received only a lukewarm response.

Duntov tried Chevrolet again after seeing the prototype Corvette at GM's Motorama auto show in January 1953.

Duntov told Hot Rod magazine's Jim Mc-Farland during a 1967 conversation that he remembered thinking "Now there's potential. I thought it wasn't a good car yet, but if you're going to do something, this looks good." A subsequent interview finally landed Duntov an engineering position at Chevrolet in May. "Not for [the] Corvette or for anything of that sort," Duntov told McFarland, "but for research and development and future stuff." Once on Chevy's payroll, Duntov wrote another letter, this one detailing his feelings about the Corvette's future. This time Cole's response to Zora's words was quick and decisive—Duntov was made a member of the Corvette engineering team, where he would stay until his retirement in 1975.

Kicking Things Off

Of course, the list of prominent players in the Corvette game's early stages did not begin nor end with Duntov. Without a doubt, Ed Cole's support for the project, first as Chevrolet's chief engineer beginning in May 1952, then as the division's

general manager and GM vice president in July 1956, was every bit as important to the Corvette's survival during those early years as Duntov's performance developments. Suspension expert Maurice Olley, then head of Chevrolet's research and development department, designed the first Corvette's chassis in 1952. Body engineer Ellis Premo oversaw the initial GRP (glass-reinforced plastic) panel designs, which were then contracted out to the Molded Fiberglass Body Company in Ashtabula, Ohio. It was Harry Barr, along with Cole, who helped breathe life into Chevrolet's aging Stovebolt six-cylinder, transforming it into the Corvette's 150hp Blue Flame six. And three-time Indianapolis 500 winner Mauri Rose was put in charge of early performance development.

General Motors styling head William L. Mitchell (left) with legendary Can-Am race driver Denny Hulme. No stranger to the track, Mitchell had first gone to work in the late 1930s as one of Harley Earl's favored stylists in Earl's Art and Colour studio. Following Earl's retirement in De-cember 1958, Mitchell became GM's top man in design and remained so for another twenty years. Along with overseeing development of Chevrolet's sensational 1963 Sting Ray, he is also credited with Buick's equally impressive 1963 Riviera.

But if any one man deserves the lion's share of the credit for the Corvette's conception, it was long-time GM styling mogul Harley Earl. As big a man as they came—both literally and figuratively—among GM's elite in the 1930s, 1940s, and 1950s, the six-foot-four Earl certainly carried considerable weight around the corporation's front office. Pushing cutting-edge projects through corporate red tape had never been a problem for him, almost from his first day on the job as a Fisher Body man in 1927.

After setting the American automotive world on its ear with his lovely, ground-breaking 1927 LaSalle—Detroit's first truly styled car—Earl was picked by GM president Alfred Sloan to head the newly created Art and Colour Section in June of that year (Art and Colour later became Styling Section in 1937). Almost overnight, Earl and his fifty-man staff catapulted GM into Detroit's styling forefront, both on the auto show circuit and down Mainstreet USA. Under his direction, Cadillacs sprouted Detroit's first tailfins in 1948, and wraparound windshields became all the rage five years later. He also created Detroit's first "dream car," the sensational Buick Y-Job, in 1938, and helped inspire the lavish Motorama auto

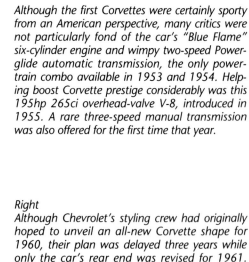

Although the first Corvettes were certainly sporty from an American perspective, many critics were not particularly fond of the car's "Blue Flame" six-cylinder engine and wimpy two-speed Powerglide automatic transmission, the only powertrain combo available in 1953 and 1954. Helping boost Corvette prestige considerably was this 195hp 265ci overhead-valve V-8, introduced in 1955. A rare three-speed manual transmission was also offered for the first time that year.

Right
Although Chevrolet's styling crew had originally hoped to unveil an all-new Corvette shape for 1960, their plan was delayed three years while only the car's rear end was revised for 1961. Clearly hinting of what buyers would see in 1963, the 1961 Corvette's new "boat-tail" rear was basically lifted off Bill Mitchell's 1958 XP-700. Notice the exposed gas cap protruding through this fuel-injected 1961 Corvette's fuel filler door—this car is equipped with the rare 24gal fiberglass fuel tank, limited-production option (LPO) number 1625.

A product of a very different time, the distinctive SR-2 Corvette was built by Chevrolet Engineering in 1956 at the request of Harley Earl. As the story goes, Earl's son Jerry wanted to race Corvettes and dad wasn't about to let him down. In all, three SR-2s were built; two racers and one street car. Originally criticized for being too heavy, Jerry Earl's SR-2 later proved itself after the younger Earl passed the car into the hands of Jim Jeffords, who won an SCCA B/Modified Production title in 1958. Here, Bud Gates pilots an SR-2 Corvette at Nassau, Bahamas, in December 1959. Dave Friedman photo

Left
A standard three-speed manual transmission, more power, an optional removable hardtop, roll-up windows, and a snazzy new shell represented big news for the fiberglass faithful in 1956. With twin four-barrel carburetors, the 1956 Corvette's 265 V-8 was rated at 210hp; adding the famed "Duntov cam," an option recommended for competition purposes only, bumped output to an unofficial 240 horses. Here, twenty-four of the 3,467 Corvettes built for 1956 pose in San Francisco.

shows, which first showcased GM's dream car lineup at New York's Waldorf-Astoria hotel in January 1949 under the "Transportation Unlimited" banner.

In the fall of 1951, Earl began thinking about producing a low-priced, sporty two-seater after toying with a pair of extravagant two-seat Buick dream cars, the LeSabre and XP-300, in 1950 and early 1951. Surrounding himself with his best people, including stylist Robert F. McLean, he somewhat secretly set out on what was perhaps his boldest venture. By April 1952, a plaster model was ready, and one look from Ed Cole a month later was enough to inspire his enthusiastic vote for continued development. Chevrolet engineers got their look at the model in June, and from there it was a mad dash to prepare the working prototype that would inspire Zora Duntov at the Waldorf-Astoria in January 1953. As intriguing as Earl's baby appeared, his Corvette show car was almost overshadowed at the 1953 Motorama by a trio of luxurious GM dreamboats, Cadillac's Eldorado, Buick's Skylark, and Oldsmobile's Fiesta. Contrary to typical Motorama show cars, all four 1953 GM droptop prototypes ended up in regular, if limited, production by the end of the year.

Improving the Breed

Corvette production began in the summer of 1953 in cramped quarters in Flint, while Chevrolet officials prepared a proper assembly line in St. Louis. Missouri manufacturing started up in December 1953, kicking off a tradition that endured until August 1981, when the revered St. Louis plant produced its last Corvette. Not long after the St. Louis assembly line started rolling, engineers began toying with a V-8 Corvette prototype in the spring of 1954. A regular-production V-8 Corvette debuted for 1955, as did an optional three-speed manual transmission, both features helping to at least minimize complaints concerning the car's original six-cylinder power and disappointing two-speed Powerglide automatic.

In 1956, Corvette news included an attractive restyle, roll-up windows, and an optional removable hardtop. A three-speed manual transmission was standard equipment behind the base 210hp 265ci V-8, which could be pumped up to 225 horses by adding the optional twin four-

Considered to be America's best race driver at the time, Indianapolis-born John Fitch was the man Chevrolet turned to in 1956 to lead its Corvette racing effort. After teaming up in February with Zora Duntov and Betty Skelton to kick up some sand at Daytona in their record-setting

Corvettes, Fitch led a four-car team to Sebring in March with meager, yet admirable results. While Duntov was busy working on his purpose-built Super Sport racer, it was Fitch who toiled over the regular-production Corvettes making them competitive on the world sports car scene.

barrel carburetors. Although recommended "for racing purposes only," Duntov's special high-lift camshaft was available under regular-production option (RPO) number 448 (or 449, depending on your source). With the famed Duntov cam, the dual-carb 265 managed an unofficial

240hp, enough to power a 1956 Corvette to 163mph during testing in Phoenix, Arizona. Impressive, but it was only the beginning.

Duntov knew the quickest way to the top of the sports car scene was through sanctioned competition, and by 1956

Chevrolet had given him leeway to promote Corvette performance as far as it would go. In February he took a three-car team to Florida for the National Association for Stock Car Automobile Racing's (NASCAR) annual Speed Week trials held on the beach at Daytona. Joining Duntov behind the wheels of the other two 1956 Corvettes were champion aerobatic pilot Betty Skelton and veteran race driver John Fitch. When the sand finally settled, Duntov had set a new sports car flying-mile record of 150.533mph, while Fitch had established a two-way average standard at 145.543mph. Skelton wasn't far behind, with a 137.773 two-way clocking.

A Fitch-led trip south for Sebring's 12-Hour competition in March wasn't as rewarding, however, a result Duntov predicted. Recognizing that straight-line speed tests and twisting, turning endurance racing represented two vastly different worlds, he wouldn't have any part of an assault on Sebring—at least not until he had a purpose-built, world-class Corvette race car capable of running long, hard, and fast with the best that Mercedes, Porsche, and Jaguar could offer.

While Duntov was at work planning just such a car, Dr. Dick Thompson, the celebrated "Flying Dentist" from Washington D.C., was busy building a Corvette racing reputation of his own, copping the first of four Sports Car Club of America (SCCA) championships in 1956. With considerable factory support from Chevrolet, Thompson's SCCA Corvettes would repeat as production-class champions in 1957, 1962, and 1963 (he garnered SCCA C-Modified honors in 1960 as well). In June 1956, he also took a turn behind the wheel of Harley Earl's finned SR-2 racer, a modified 1956 Corvette built for Earl's son Jerry. One of three SR-2s produced (two competition versions, one street model), Jerry Earl's racer ended up

Left
After receiving quad headlights in 1958, Corvettes were basically unchanged up front through 1962 when the last of the solid-rear-axle, convertible-only models were built. In 1962, one year before the totally new Sting Ray coupe made the scene, Corvette sales had jumped nearly 40 percent to an all-time high of 14,531 units. Wide whitewalls on this 1962 Corvette are incorrect.

Zora Duntov poses proudly in his Super Sport racer, XP-64, at Sebring in March 1957. Eschewing a role in Chevrolet's 1956 attempt at racing glory in Florida, Duntov saw no reason to waste his efforts on the stock Corvette with its excessive weight and substandard brakes. In his mind, the only way to beat the Europeans at Sebring—or hopefully Le Mans—was to specially build a racing Corvette from the ground up. With a tube frame, four-wheel independent suspension, finned drum brakes (mounted inboard on the differential housing) and a lightweight magnesium frame, the 1957 SS was certainly a purpose-built racer. Overheating problems, however, doomed the car to failure at Sebring in March 1957, then the infamous AMA factory racing "ban" killed the project entirely later that spring.

Washington D.C.'s famed "Flying Dentist," Dr. Dick Thompson, was easily the most successful Corvette race driver in the 1950s and early 1960s. Even after the AMA ban supposedly had closed the door between Detroit and the track in 1957, Thompson continued receiving considerable support from Chevrolet, with the result being a steady string of victories in Sports Car Club of America competition. Thompson took turns behind the wheels of, among others, Harley Earl's SR-2, Bill Mitchell's Stingray, and Zora Duntov's Grand Sport. He won SCCA titles in various classes in 1956, 1957, and 1960–1962.

taking the SCCA B-Modified Production title in 1958 with Jim Jeffords driving for Chicago's Nickey Chevrolet.

As for street-going Corvettes, buyers in 1957 were treated to various exciting, new options, including a four-speed manual transmission and Ramjet fuel injection. Designed by Duntov at Ed Cole's request and supplied by Rochester, the Ramjet unit helped the Corvette's newly enlarged 283ci V-8 reach the magical one-horsepower-per-cubic-inch level in top-performance trim. Along with the exceptional 283hp 283 "fuelie," Corvette customers in 1957 could also add wider wheels, heavy-duty suspension, and beefy brakes featuring finned drums, ceramic-metallic linings, and special cooling ducts. A very rare oversized fuel tank was produced as well, although the few released undoubtedly went right into racers' hands.

Back on the track, 1957 also marked the debut of the first of Duntov's "dream" Corvettes, the Super Sport racer. First fashioned in clay in July 1956, the SS was intended to take Sebring by storm, and might have done just that had more time been invested in the project. Exceptionally innovative features included a fuel-injected 283 V-8 with aluminum heads, a tubular space frame, a lightweight magnesium body, coilover shock suspension, and a servo-controlled brake booster system designed to prevent the rear drums from locking up during hard stops.

Two Super Sports were built—a white fiberglass test "mule" and the beautiful blue, magnesium-bodied Sebring challenger—and both were hastily rushed to Florida before the bugs could be ironed out. SS power was certainly up to speed, as the mule proved during practice laps. Brakes, however, were far from adequate. And as John Fitch discovered during his short time in the blue SS, the magnesium shell couldn't dissipate heat like its fiberglass counterpart. All that fuel-injected might was wasted as Duntov's hopes for success at Sebring literally melted away after only twenty-two laps. Although Duntov regrouped with his sights set on Le Mans, the rug was pulled out from under him before the Super Sport team could take another shot at international racing glory.

By 1957, many among Detroit's auto-making elite had seen enough of the so-called horsepower race. Some believed performance had been promoted to unsafe levels, while underlying feelings questioned the logic of factory racing teams competing against their own customers running privately. Finally fed up, the Automobile Manufacturers Association (AMA) in June agreed to stop such shenanigans. The AMA statement read as follows:

"Whereas, the Automobile Manufacturers Association believes that the automobile manufacturers should encourage owners and drivers to evaluate passenger cars in terms of useful power and ability to provide safe, reliable, and comfortable transportation, rather than in terms of capacity for speed. Now, therefore, this board unanimously recommends to the member companies engaged in the manufacture and sale of passenger cars and station wagons that they:

"Not participate or engage in any public contest, competitive event or test of passenger cars involving or suggesting racing or speed, including acceleration tests, or encourage or furnish financial, engineering, manufacturing, advertising, or public relations assistance, or supply 'pace cars' or 'official cars,' in connection with any such contest, event, or test, directly or indirectly.

"Not participate or engage in, or encourage or assist employees, dealers, or others in the advertising or publicizing of (a) any race or speed contest, test or competitive event involving or suggesting speed, whether public or private, involving passenger cars or the results thereof; or (b) the actual or comparative capabilities of passenger cars for speed, or the specific engine size, torque, horsepower or ability to accelerate or perform in any context that suggests speed."

Well aware of what was coming, Chevrolet's braintrust torpedoed the Super Sport project a few months before the AMA verdict came down. While the so-called "ban" on factory racing and performance did cool things off considerably, GM's back door remained open to certain prominent racers. Winners like Dick Thompson continued receiving covert factory support, and much of the race-bred equipment—heavy-duty suspension pieces, metallic brakes, fuel injection, oversized fuel tanks, and so on—stayed on the Corvette options list through the 1950s.

Duntov's Super Sport carried on, too, though in another form. Late in 1958, GM styling chief William Mitchell—who had just replaced Harley Earl at the top following Earl's retirement—obtained the SS mule's chassis, then used it as base for a private race car. In keeping with the AMA ban, at least as far as the public was concerned, Chevrolet made it clear to any and all innocent bystanders that Mitchell was to use his own resources to campaign the ensuing "Stingray" racer, a machine *he* reportedly owned, not Chevrolet. As Allan Girdler later wrote in *Road & Track*, "Mitchell somehow managed to get title to [the SS] chassis signed over to him. Heck, yes, it was a political thing, and it probably didn't fool anybody but the point was Mitchell was allowed to have the best guys in the shop work on his racing car, all for experimental purposes and/or as a hobby, ho ho."

Rebodied with a sleek, sexy fiberglass shell, Mitchell's "hobby racer" more than hinted at things to come in 1963, and not in name alone. As for its abilities at the track, the first Stingray was an easy SCCA C-Modified class champion in 1960 with the ever-present Dr. Dick Thompson at the wheel.

Compared to Earl's SR-2, Duntov's SS, and Mitchell's Stingray, regular-production Corvette advances during the late 1950s were relatively ho-hum. Top engine output did increase over that span, but the same small-block V-8 (283ci from 1957 to 1961; 327ci in 1962) tied to a solid rear axle prevailed in typical Yankee meat-and-potatoes fashion. Major styling changes were limited to the addition of quad headlights (1958) and Bill Mitchell's ducktail rear (1961), the latter inspired by Mitchell's XP-700 prototype of 1958.

That the Corvette carried on in such similar fashion from 1958 to 1962 was grounds enough to help inspire alarm among the fiberglass faithful upon witnessing the transformation made in 1963. That that transformation still stands today as one of the most stunning automotive renditions in this or any other country's history only helps make the legend loom larger. With breathtaking styling and an excellent chassis featuring innovative independent rear suspension, the 1963 Sting Ray emerged as the greatest Corvette to that point. Looking back at the original 1953 Corvette, it was hard to believe only ten years separated the two. And from today's perspective, it's nearly as tough to accept that the Sting Ray is now thirty years old. A timeless classic? You decide.

Although Chevrolet's movers and shakers probably relied on that same beautiful body one year too long, it

Veteran Mechanix Illustrated *writer Tom McAhill (left) checks out the new fuel-injected Corvette with Zora Duntov. Introduced for 1957, the Rochester-built Ramjet injection unit helped put the Corvette into another league of performance, though early bugs often left many "fuelie" owners on the bench. In top form, a 1957 fuel-injected 283 V-8 was rated at 283hp. Chevrolet bragged of having the first engine to produce one horsepower per cubic inch, but Chrysler had actually been the first the year before with its 355hp 354 hemi, a brute of an engine offered as an option for the equally brutish 300B luxury performance bomb.*

wasn't like they were beating a dead horse. Even though the nameplate was used through 1976 (as one word after 1969), whether someone says "Stingray" or "Sting Ray," most red-blooded Americans automatically think of the Corvettes built between 1963 and 1967.

21

Chapter Two

1963

The Sting Ray Makes Its Splash

As much as it looked like Chevrolet's Corvette was all but dead after 1954, Ed Cole and crew were, in fact, regrouping for a second shot at breaking into the sports car game. While purists scoffed at the Powerglide automatic, Europeans laughed at the somewhat thinly disguised Stovebolt six, and pampered Americans questioned the crude soft top and side curtains, Cole was busy paying close attention to what was going on in Dearborn. If any one thing saved the first Corvette from a quick death, it was the appearance in 1954 of a prototype Thunderbird, a wonderfully sporty luxury toy loaded with amenities, as well as V-8 power. Although Ford's two-seater was a different breed, Chevrolet wasn't about to be one-upped, and from there the sky became the limit. Introducing Chevy's new over-head-valve V-8 between fiberglass fenders in 1955 was only the beginning.

Corvette popularity began to soar once the Duntov factor entered the equation and a fresh fiberglass form made the scene in 1956. With that new body, a better chassis, some serious V-8 power, and a few added "luxuries" such as roll-up windows and an optional removable hardtop, almost overnight the 1956 Corvette silenced critics and brought raves from buyers. Production of America's only sports car jumped to 3,467 in 1956, nearly doubled to 6,339 in 1957, surpassed the 10,000 unit level in 1960, and reached 14,531 in 1962. GM's front office seemed satisfied with such success, especially considering the Corvette's relatively tight market niche. Duntov, however, was never quite happy, at least not as far as his goal of building a supreme sports car was concerned.

By 1960, kibitzers in this country were no longer questioning the Corvette's status as a sports car, thanks in part to several victorious SCCA racing campaigns, most notably Dr. Dick Thompson's. Nonetheless, Duntov's high-flying ideals still dominated his thinking. Winning races at Riverside in California or Elkhart Lake in Wisconsin certainly did a lot for the Corvette image, but in Duntov's mind the only avenue to real glory was the Mulsanne Straight in France, the famed high-speed stretch at Le Mans. America's sports car? Zora wanted a *world* sports car, an agile, high-powered performance machine capable of beating Europe's best on their own turf.

Even with the performance advancements made beginning in 1956, Duntov and his engineering crew knew they could never reach such a lofty goal with the existing Corvette design. Power was plentiful, but a proliferation of mundane pas-

When first listed, RPO Z06 was priced at roughly $1,800. Once the oversized fuel tank and still-born knock-off wheels were dropped from the package, the price was lowered to a tad less than $1,300. Production of 1963 Z06 coupes was only 199. The Sebring Silver paint on this Z06 Sting Ray was an extra-cost option priced at $80.70. Listed under RPO number 941, Sebring Silver paint was chosen by 3,516 Corvette buyers in 1963.

Corvettes had been nearly unbeatable in SCCA production-class competition in 1960, 1961, and most of 1962. But just when it looked like the new 1963 Z06 Sting Ray would help continue the clean sweep, a little Anglo-American hybrid racer built by Carroll Shelby using Ford's Windsor small-block V-8 entered the picture. Both cars, Chevrolet's Z06 and Shelby's 260 Cobra, debuted at Riverside, California, in October 1962, and though Chevrolet won the first battle, Shelby quickly dominated the war. Here Shelby-American pilot Ken Miles' Cobra leads long-time Corvette racer Bob Bondurant's 1963 Z06 Sting Ray at Dodger Stadium in February 1963. This was a view that would become all too common for Chevrolet competitors as the Cobra supplanted the Corvette as America's top sports racer. Dave Friedman photo

senger-car suspension components hindered ride and handling, especially in back where a solid rear axle limited per-

formance developments. Brakes never had been up to snuff, and weight posed an ever-present problem; not only were early Corvettes too heavy relative to international rivals, but they also were balanced improperly, in Zora's opinion, with about 53 percent of total weight resting on their front wheels. As Duntov had learned from Germany's dominating mid-engined Auto Union race cars of the 1930s, a rearward weight bias greatly assisted traction and lightened steering effort. By his estimates, a 40/60 (percentage, front and rear) weight distribution was preferred, though attaining such a ratio was next to impossible with a heavy V-8 sitting between a car's front wheels.

Although Duntov's first attempt at building the supreme Corvette, his SS racer of 1957, saw the engine mounted up front in typical fashion, its super light-

weight body and tubular frame suspended independently at all four corners did represent state-of-the-art design. After the infamous AMA ban of June 1957 snuffed out the SS project before it could prove itself at Le Mans, Duntov began rethinking his approach. In 1958, his thoughts turned seriously to a mid-engined layout, an idea he would campaign right up to his retirement in 1975. (Chevrolet officials finally squelched his mid-engined Corvette proposals in 1974.)

Early inspiration for Duntov's dreams of a mid-engined Corvette came in the form of the stillborn Q-Corvette. Initially involving a Chevrolet passenger-car proposal made in 1957, the Q-code project featured an innovative rear-transaxle layout with independent suspension and inboard drum brakes. By moving the transmission to the rear while the engine stayed up front, designers at least had gained ground, however minimal, toward a preferred weight distribution. Independent rear suspension and inboard brakes also greatly reduced unsprung weight, the prime negative aspect of the age-old solid rear axle setup.

Too much unsprung weight (the mass not supported by the springs, such as tires, wheels, brake components, differential, axle housing, and so on) relative to the amount of sprung weight (body, frame, engine and transmission, passengers, fuel, luggage) translates into severe vertical wheel motion under harsh driving conditions (road bumps, hard acceleration, radical direction changes). Simply put, the mass of sprung weight must be substantial enough to dampen the unsprung mass' natural tendency to react proportionally to uneven road surfaces, changing loads during cornering, and inadequate traction. Reducing unsprung weight not only helps handling, but it also greatly improves general ride quality.

Such was the aim of the Q-code project, originally slated as the new Chevrolet for 1960. Of course, the project's performance potential couldn't be overlooked, and it almost immediately became the platform for an all-new Corvette also proposed for 1960. Duntov penned the Q-Corvette's unit-body chassis on an extremely short 94in wheelbase, down eight inches from the standard model, while stylist Bob McLean fashioned a sleek, low coupe body standing only 46in tall. Planned for production in steel, McLean's startling shell debuted full-scale in clay in November 1957. Slim, flowing, and compact with "pop-up" headlights, a pointed fastback roofline, and stylish bulges atop each wheel opening, it was a look that would survive even though the Q-Corvette wouldn't. Although the front-engined, rear-transaxle arrangement would appear beneath the skin of Pontiac's new Tempest in 1961, Chevrolet quickly gave up on the Q concept once retooling costs were determined to be too great.

Hopes for an all-new, world-class Corvette were temporarily derailed, therefore, leaving Duntov to his drawing board. He admitted that the proposed rear-transaxle layout still hadn't done enough, in his mind, toward a better balanced Corvette. Yet at the same time, he

Although it was a little overdone up front and a lot gaudy overall, Bill Mitchell's 1958 XP-700 did lay the groundwork for the 1961 Corvette's restyled rear end, which in turn carried over basically intact into the Sting Ray era.

Bill Mitchell's private race car, the XP87 Stingray, was built in the winter of 1958–59 using the 1957 Super Sport mule's chassis. Both a familiar styling exercise and a successful racer, Mitchell's Stingray was driven by Dr. Dick Thompson to an SCCA C/Modified Production title in 1960. Following its retirement from the track, the Stingray took to the showcar circuit, debuting at Chicago's McCormick Place on February 18, 1961.

also recognized the budgetary realities—made even more crucial by the impending national recession of 1958—common to all of Detroit's auto makers. Concerning future Corvettes, Duntov wrote the following memo to engineer Harry Barr in December 1957:

We can attempt to arrive at the general concept of the car on the basis of our experience, and in relationship to the present Corvette. We would like to have better driver and passenger accommodation, better luggage space, better ride, better

handling, and higher performance. Superficially, it would seem that the comfort requirements indicate a larger car than the present Corvette. However, this is not so. With a new chassis concept and thoughtful body engineering and styling, the car may be bigger internally and somewhat smaller [externally] than the present Corvette. Consideration of cost spells the use of a large number of passenger car components which indicates that the chassis cannot become so small that [those components] cannot be used.

Cost-consciousness notwithstanding, Duntov's next major engineering experiment ran about as far from regular-production realities as it could possibly get. With the Q-Corvette gone, he refocused his efforts in 1959 on mid-engined designs, resulting in his first Chevrolet Experimental Research Vehicle. Appropriately named CERV I (CERV II would appear in 1963, CERV III in 1990), Duntov's open-wheel follow-up to his ill-fated Super Sport made its public debut at Riverside, California, in November 1960 looking every bit like an Indy-style race car even though Chevrolet was notably not in the business of building race cars. Accordingly, official press releases diplomatically described the machine as "a research tool for Chevrolet's continuous investigations into automotive ride and handling phenomena under the most realistic conditions."

Along with its aluminum V-8 mounted directly behind the driver, innovative CERV I features included a tubular space frame, a specially constructed lightweight fiberglass body, and independent rear suspension (IRS) with inboard aluminum drum brakes. Similar to the design proposed for the Q-Corvette, the CERV I's IRS setup—the work of Duntov and his senior engineers, Harold Krieger and Walt

Zetye—was of a relàtively simple three-link arrangement using the U-jointed half-shafts as the upper locating link. Typical chrome-moly tubes took care of lower linking chores, while a boxed-steel combination hub-carrier, radius-arm on each side made up the all-important horizontal third link, the point where forward thrust was transmitted to the frame.

Whether or not the mid-engined CERV I could have proven its merits at the track is anyone's guess. Despite hints at a possible Indy 500 entry, GM officials never would have allowed such behavior, leaving the vehicle to do its "research tool" thing in private. As a consolation of sorts, at least it did do that job well. Like McLean's Q-Corvette body, the CERV I's IRS pieces would come in handy soon enough.

By 1960, work on an honest-to-goodness all-new regular-production Corvette was indeed under way. While Duntov had been busy toying with his mid-engined ideals, Bill Mitchell's stylists had been hard at work envisioning a more readily acceptable future for Chevrolet's fiberglass two-seater. Mitchell, a Harley Earl protégé who went to work for the famed finman at his Art and Colour Studio in the late 1930s, had been picked by the retiring Earl as his successor atop GM Styling in December 1958. Almost immediately, Mitchell made his first contribution to the next-generation Corvette, "borrowing" much of the Q-Corvette's shape for his Stingray race car built that winter.

Young Larry Shinoda, at work at GM Styling for barely a year, was most responsible for the Stingray's stunning lines, a thoroughly modern look that Mitchell and his crew knew would become the new Corvette's image. Their first attempt to transform that look into a production reality as a facelift for 1962 failed miserably during the winter of 1958–1959. More successful, however, was Mitchell's XP-700 prototype, built that previous summer. A bit far-fetched up front, the 1958 XP-700 featured a much more pleasant ducktail rear end, a shape that *was* accepted as a standard Corvette styling revision for 1961.

That year, Mitchell also had Shinoda design yet another Corvette show car, the XP-755, called the Shark. Although many felt the Shark—later renamed the Mako Shark I—was a precursor to the all-new

Larry Shinoda, shown here in January 1993 at the annual Corvette extravaganza held at Cypress Gardens, Florida, penned the 1963 Sting Ray's stunning lines, as he had Bill Mitchell's Stingray racer, built during the winter of 1958-59. During his stay at GM Styling from 1956 to 1968, Shinoda also had a hand in the design of both the CERV I and CERV II, Mitchell's Shark (later renamed Mako Shark I) and Mako Shark II, the rear-engined XP-819, and various mid-engined Corvette prototypes. In 1968, he defected from GM to Ford, following his boss, Bunkie Knudsen. In a somewhat odd twist of fate, Shinoda found himself designing the image for Ford's famed Boss 302 Mustang not long after he had helped create Chevrolet's Z/28 Camaro, both cars ending up as heated rivals on the SCCA Trans-Am circuit.

Corvette to come, it was actually a copy, its lines being drawn directly from the regular-production prototype already well under way at the time. XP-755 was a personal flight of fancy for Bill Mitchell; the true working model for future development was the XP-720, born earlier in the fall of 1959 in a cramped basement area known as Studio X.

Shinoda, again, did the sketchwork for the XP-720 project. And after watching his proposal for a mid-engined Q-Corvette follow-up fall by the wayside the previous year, Duntov then supplied a suitably advanced front-engined chassis to match the XP-720's wonderfully modern coupe

Left

Larry Shinoda's touch was clearly present from any angle on the all-new 1963 Corvette Sting Ray. As Hot Rod's *Ray Brock wrote, "those who may have seen the experimental Stingray in action the past couple of years will immediately note a strong resemblance." Shinoda had designed Bill Mitchell's Stingray in 1958, and much of that look carried over five years later. Base price for a 1963 Sting Ray coupe was $4,257. Production was 10,594.*

This April 1960 Larry Shinoda sketch depicts the CERV I racer, which debuted at Riverside in November 1960. Its mid-engine design was just the layout Zora Duntov had in mind for the future

Corvette of his dreams. As it was, that idea was a dead end, but the CERV I's innovative three-link IRS setup would find its way beneath the regular-production 1963 Sting Ray.

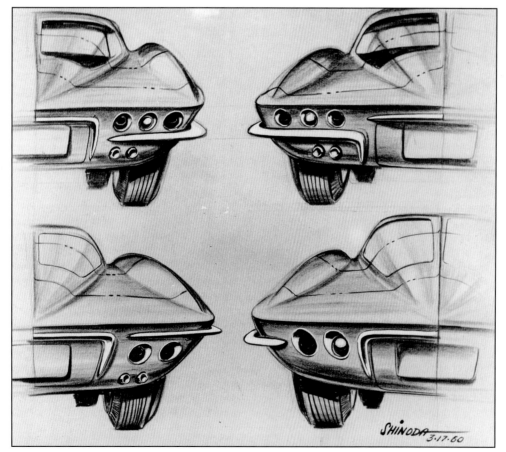

body. Once refined, the XP-720 prototype did indeed became a production reality, with Chevrolet's long-awaited redesigned Corvette hitting showrooms in both traditional convertible and welcomed coupe forms in the fall of 1962.

"For the last five years, we've been bombarded with rumors of an 'all-new' Corvette that was supposed to be just around the corner," wrote Roger Huntington in *Motor Trend*'s January 1963 issue. "It was going to feature just about everything that was new and exciting in modern sports car design. We waited anxiously." From an automotive journalist's perspective, the waiting ended in June 1962, when Chevrolet unveiled its startling Sting Ray coupe for the press at GM's Milford Proving Grounds. Rave reviews quickly followed.

"This is the one we've been waiting for," gushed Huntington. "And it's all the rumors promised—and more. This is a *modern* sports car. In most ways it's as advanced as the latest dual-purpose sports/luxury cars from Europe—and this includes the new Jaguar XK-E, Ferrari GT, Mercedes 300-SL, and all the rest. The new Corvette doesn't have to take a back seat to any of them, in looks, performance, handling, or ride." Although considerable ink would flow in praise of the 1963 Sting Ray, perhaps its arrival was best summed up by Zora Duntov himself after the car's introduction to the press: "For the first time I now have a Corvette I can be proud to drive in Europe."

No stone was left unturned during the Corvette's total transformation from uniquely American sportster to world-class legend, beginning with Shinoda's sexy Sting Ray shell. Revered for its low, lovely lines, as well as its ground-breaking status as Chevrolet's first closed Corvette, the 1963 Sting Ray coupe was exceptionally modern looking, sleek, and compact, measuring nearly three inches lower, three and one-half inches thinner side-to-side, and two inches shorter than its 1958–62 forerunners. Wheelbase was also

Left
These Shinoda sketches, dated March 17, 1960, show differing approaches to taillight and bumper layouts. Interestingly, the triple taillight arrangements appearing in the top two drawings became a popular customizer's trick not long after the 1963 Sting Ray hit the streets.

down, from the traditional 102in to 98in, and both front and rear tracks were narrowed slightly.

Even with these reductions, interior room and comfort were improved, thanks to, among other things, a lower floor and repositioned bucket seats. Although forward and aft travel of the buckets was a meager four inches, legroom was relatively substantial, more so for the driver since the engine and transmission were located one inch to the right. And as the 1963 owners manual explained, "additional adjustments to tailor the seat location to your personal requirements can be performed by your Chevrolet Dealer." Backrest angle could be changed mechanically as well, as could seat height, through a maximum range of about one and one-quarter inches. Impressed by these surroundings, *Hot Rod*'s Ray Brock wrote: "The first thing we noticed about the

1963 Corvette was that you feel at home the minute you slip behind the wheel. Our former Corvette tests always required a 'break-in' period to get accustomed to the seating and steering. Not so this one—you feel at ease immediately. A few sharp turns later and you know you've found a friend."

Back on the outside, muscular wheel bulges at all four corners and the prominent break line running completely around the body were, by no coincidence, particularly reminiscent of Mitchell's Stingray racer, as were the twin dummy hood vents. Original plans to make the 1963 Sting Ray's vents functional, like the Stingray's, were reportedly dropped to prevent hot underhood air from flowing directly into the passenger compartment's cowl intakes.

Q-Corvette ties were also prominent in the form of the tapered fastback roof

and hideaway headlights up front. Representing Detroit's first use of hidden headlights since Chrysler Corporation's 1942 DeSoto, the Sting Ray's "flip-up" design required more than its fair share of midnight oil, with five different systems tried before a suitable electrical mechanism was perfected.

As for the tapered roof, it was an extension of Mitchell's "stinger" concept, a Sting Ray styling queue that began as a blade-shape bulge (Mitchell's "phallic symbol," in Shinoda's words) running from nose to cowl, then carried over the

Ed Cole briefly pushed for this four-place Sting Ray, a model that fortunately never survived past the prototype stage. Looking definitely ungainly on a stretched wheelbase, this enlarged Corvette earned a thumbs down from Bill Mitchell and Zora Duntov.

roof down to the tail in the form of a raised ridge. Along the way, that ridge parted the rear glass area into two sections, resulting in the renown "split-window" theme. An obvious case of function falling victim to form, Mitchell's split-window idea didn't work at all for Duntov, who questioned its negative impact on rearward visibility. GM's styling guru, however, was adamant. "If you take that off," said Mitchell, "you might as well forget the whole thing." The stinger stayed, but Duntov didn't forget.

Shinoda's attractive new body also featured aircraft-style doors cut into the roofline to aid entry and exit. Yet another aircraft-inspired design trick helped freshen up the basic form that Shinoda had first penned five years before. Aeronautical engineers had discovered in the 1950s that adding a "pinched waistline" to a fighter jet's fuselage was a key to maximizing supersonic flight envelopes; by doing the same thing to the 1963 Sting Ray shell—letting the front and rear quarters bulge outward slightly in relation to the doors—Shinoda updated the image he had originally helped create for the Stingray racer.

From a wind-cheating perspective, however, the all-new Corvette looked more supersonic that it actually was.

Left
Four 327ci V-8s were available for the 1963 Sting Ray. The top carbureted Corvette engine option in 1963 was RPO L76, the 340hp 327. Sharing a Carter AFB four-barrel carburetor with the L75 300hp 327 (the base 250hp 327 was equipped with a smaller Carter four-barrel), the L76 had solid lifters and 11.25:1 compression. The L75 had hydraulic lifters and 10.5:1 compression. Unique to the L76 was the louvered, round air cleaner, while the finned valve covers were also used on the L84 fuel-injected 327. Price for this L76 327 was $107.60; the milder L75 cost $53.80.

Below
Bill Mitchell turned to stylist Larry Shinoda once more in 1961, directing him to copy the basic lines of the XP-720 Sting Ray prototype and create a personal car for Mitchell himself. Completed in a few months, XP-755, the so-called "Shark," was painted, at Mitchell's request, to match the ocean predator for which it was named. When Mitchell again asked Shinoda to apply a similar finish to another Corvette prototype in 1965, XP-755 was renamed the Mako Shark I as that new car became the Mako Shark II—an experimental model that lead the way for the coming of the redesigned 1968 Corvette.

Wind-tunnel testing under the direction of Dr. Peter Kyropoulos at the California Institute of Technology demonstrated that, like the SS and Stingray racers, the 1963 Sting Ray was a real "lifter," as Duntov called it. Aerodynamically, the new Corvette did offer considerably less frontal area (meaning less drag) compared to its predecessors, but that age-old problem of high-speed lift caused by air pressure build-up beneath the car wasn't solved.

Nonetheless, the 1963 Sting Ray coupe body was light-years ahead of previous Corvette designs, thanks in part to assistant staff engineer Walter Horner. Stouter, yet lighter, the all-new shell featured Horner's reinforced steel "birdcage" beneath all that fiberglass, a development that helped guarantee a sure, solid feel. The Sting Ray's welded "birdcage" weighed eighty–two pounds, compared to the 1962 Corvette, which had forty-

eight pounds of steel reinforcement. But its added strength meant less fiberglass was required—with a convertible version of the birdcage reinforcement, a 1963 droptop weighed 397 pounds, down eight pounds from 1962.

On the other hand, overall weight wasn't much less than in 1962, despite a reduction in every exterior dimension, a fact that greatly disappointed Duntov. Helping make the 1963 Sting Ray heavier than planned was, among other things, the hideaway headlight system, beefier exhaust pipes with thickened walls for increased durability, a 20gal gas tank in place of the previous 16gal unit, and bigger brakes. Duntov's totally redesigned chassis may have appeared heavier, but like the reinforced body atop it, his new frame greatly improved the Corvette's rigidity without a typical corresponding increase in weight.

The Sting Ray's ladder-type frame design differed greatly from the antiquated X-member frame used under all previous Corvettes, offering 50 percent more torsional stiffness while weighing in at 260

Standard power in 1963 came from this 250hp 327 backed by a Saginaw three-speed manual transmission. Like the optional L75 327, the base small-block featured 10.5:1 compression and hydraulic lifters. Also common to both the 250- and 300-horse 327s were painted valve covers and a dual-snorkel air cleaner. Only 18 percent of Sting Ray buyers stayed with the base 327 in 1963, while a mere 919 buyers—4 percent—chose the standard three-speed manual transmission. The most popular power option was the L75 327, with 8,033 sold. Favorite optional drivetrain features included the M20 four-speed and G81 Positraction differential—84 percent of 1963 Corvette customers opted for RPO M20 and 82 percent picked RPO G81.

The Sting Ray frame's widely spaced perimeter rails meant the car's passenger compartment could lie down between those rails, which in turn translated into a truly low roofline (49.6in) without sacrificing headroom. Also notice the exhaust pipes running through the transmission cross-member (just below the steering column in this view)—a necessity to insure ample ground clearance. Another innovation was the adjustable steering column, which could be relocated mechanically (from under the hood) in or out up to three inches.

pounds, same as the discarded 1962 design. Five cross-members tied together the two boxed perimeter rails, which were widely spaced to allow the interior floor pan to drop between them, meaning the design crew could lower the 1963 Corvette's roofline dramatically without reducing headroom. The second cross-member from the front incorporated a pair of tubular inserts that made room for

the exhaust pipes to run up close to the floor pan, a necessity as far as suitable ground clearance was concerned. Cross-member number three included a slight recess on top where the driveshaft ran *above* it. Member number three also worked in concert with number four atop the frame's kicked-up tail section as mounting points for the Sting Ray's innovative independent rear suspension.

IRS advantages include the obvious ability of both wheels to respond independently to changing road conditions. Depending on the design, an IRS setup also can be adjusted for negative camber, meaning the tires lean in slightly on top. Negative camber translates into better adhesion for the outside tire during hard cornering since more of the tread remains planted as the car rolls away from the turn. Standard solid axle suspensions tend to lift the tread's "footprint" off the road during hard turns as the outside rear tire

is forced to lean out; needless to say, the first and foremost requirement for good handling is to keep as much tread as possible on the road at all times. IRS designs also considerably reduce unsprung weight compared to solid rear axles since only the tires, wheels, and brakes are suspended by the springs.

Duntov had been well aware of the advantages of IRS, having first tried the idea on his Super Sport race car in 1957. But the SS used a somewhat antiquated, European-style DeDion rear axle. A more advanced, relatively simple three-link IRS arrangement was Duntov's choice for the CERV I, and it was that experimental arrangement that laid the groundwork for the Sting Ray's design.

Similar in form to the CERV I setup save for springing, the 1963 Sting Ray's IRS relied on each U-jointed halfshaft as upper locating links from the differential to the hubs. Typical control rods made up the lateral lower links from differential to hub carriers, which came at the end of a pair of boxed-steel trailing arms that supplied the longitudinal third link to the frame on each side. Space constraints ruled out the CERV I's coilover shocks, forcing the engineering team to use what Duntov called an "anachronistic feature"—a transverse multi-leaf spring mounted below and behind the differential. Undoubtedly representing the only feature a Model T and a Corvette ever shared, that nine-leaf transverse spring may have appeared out of place, but it did the job it had to do in lieu of the more expensive coilovers.

Typical full-sized Chevrolet suspension components (unequal-length A-arms with coil springs) were used up front, as they had been since 1953, to help keep a lid on production costs. But as part of the Corvette package, the standard A-arms were located differently to raise the Sting Ray's front roll center, which translated into less tire lean in relation to body roll during hard turns, which in turn meant more tread on the road. Other modifications included moving the steering linkage from ahead of the suspension arms, where it resided in passenger-car applications, to behind. Steering itself was greatly improved as the worm-and-sector steering box used in 1962 was replaced by a new recirculating-ball setup.

Sting Ray owners could also choose between two steering ratios, the standard 20.2:1 or a faster 17.6:1. Previous Corvette quick-steering options relied on a bolt-on adapter that adjusted the steering gear geometry at a point where the tie-rods joined in the middle. All 1963 Sting Rays were delivered with two holes drilled in each spindle's steering arm. Turning to the faster ratio was as easy as unbolting the tie-rod ends from the standard "setting" and moving them to the holes closer to the spindle. Steering wheel turns lock-to-lock were 3.4 for the standard ratio, 2.92 for the quicker setting. Yet another mechanical adjustment, this one found under the hood, could telescope the steering column, moving the steering wheel in or out up to three inches to suit the driver.

Sting Ray brakes were improved 18 percent by adding wider drums all around. In front, the 11x2in drums used in 1962 were replaced by 11x2.75in units, while the rears went from 11x1.75in to 11x2in, translating to an increase in total swept area from 259sq-in to 328. New brake equipment also included a self-adjusting feature (engaged in reverse) and optional power assist, RPO J50, priced at $43.05. Optional power steering, RPO N40, was offered to Corvette buyers for the first time in 1963. The N40 price tag was $75.35.

Overall, the 1963 Sting Ray chassis represented a marked improvement in every respect. Although they still left ample room for improvement, the bigger brakes were welcomed. Steering was more precise and ride was softer, thanks mostly to the reduction in unsprung weight in back; roughly 300 pounds for the 1962 Corvette's solid rear axle setup compared to only 200 pounds for the Sting Ray's IRS. The total ratio of sprung to unsprung weight increased considerably from 5.27:1 in 1962 to 7.98:1. Referring to that improvement, *Motor Trend's* Roger Huntington pointed out that "many Corvette owners use the car as they would a Thunderbird—as a two-seater personal car. These people want a plush ride. The early Corvette wasn't bad in this department, but this new one is unbelievable for a car of its weight and wheelbase."

Even though Duntov's dream of a mid-engined Corvette had remained just that, he did manage to favorably redistribute the car's weight by shifting the powertrain and passenger compartment rearward on the Sting Ray's shortened wheelbase. A more acceptable 48/52 weight bias, combined with less unsprung mass, improved both handling and off-the-line capabilities. Not only could the new Sting Ray go around corners better than any Corvette yet, it also could launch out of the hole unlike any of its forerunners.

Although some may have initially scoffed at the Sting Ray's transverse "buggy spring," there was nothing funny about the way this IRS layout performed. With the center section bolted to the frame through rubber bushings, total unsprung weight was down considerably compared to the conventional solid rear axle used in 1962. A simple three-link design, the Corvette's IRS setup used each half-shaft as an upper locating link. Typical control rods made up the lower links, while the horizontal trailing arm hub carriers completed the triangle.

Standard Sting Ray interior features included a color-keyed, plastic-rimmed steering wheel; a 160-mph speedometer; and a 7000-rpm tachometer. Tachs differed depending on engine choice. The two hydraulic-lifter 327s, the base 250hp version and the optional 300hp L75, came with tach faces showing an orange band from 5000 to 5300rpm and a red band from 5300 to 5500rpm. The mechanical-cam engines, the 340hp L76 and 360hp L84 fuelie, were equipped with a tach showing an orange band from 6300 to 6500rpm and a redline beginning at 6500rpm. Interior trim colors of black, red, saddle, or blue were offered. The leather seats shown here were an $80.70 option picked by 1,334 buyers in 1963.

The star of the Z06 show was the special heavy-duty brake package included as part of the deal. Linings were sintered "cerametalix" while the enlarged drums were finned for cooling. Also helping keep things cool were internal "fans," screened backing plates with "elephant ear" air scoops, and special openings in the drums' faces.

A Z06 Corvette was equipped with the top performance powerplant available in 1963, the L84 fuel-injected 327, rated at 360hp. Only one transmission, the close-ratio Muncie four-speed, was bolted up to the L84 when RPO Z06 was selected. The base three-speed was available behind the 360hp 327 in non-Z06 cars, as it was with the L76 small-block, though only fifty-nine such combinations (both L76 and L84) were sold. Notice the power brake booster and dual-circuit master cylinder at the top of the photo; it's a combination unique to the Z06 options group. Priced at a healthy $430.40, RPO L84 was checked off by 2,610 Corvette buyers in 1963.

Contrary to all the changes made, 1963 horsepower numbers carried over unchanged from 1962. Standard Sting Ray power came from a 250hp 327ci V-8 fed by a single Carter WCFB four-barrel carburetor and backed by a Saginaw three-speed manual transmission sending torque to 3.36:1 gears in back. A Positraction differential (RPO G81) was available at extra cost ($43.05), as were various gear ratios running from a 3.08:1 Special Highway Axle to a 4.56:1 stump puller. Optional engines included three more 327 small-blocks: 300 and 340hp versions, both with Carter AFB four-barrels, and the top-dog 360hp variety, RPO L84, with the potent, yet fussy Rochester fuel injection. Hydraulic cams and 10.5:1 compression were features of the standard 327 and 300hp L75 V-8, while the higher performance 340hp L76 and 360hp L84 fuelie got solid-lifter cams and 11.25:1 compression.

The aging two-speed Powerglide automatic transmission (M35) was an op-

tion behind the 250 and 300hp 327s. Two optional Borg-Warner T-10 four-speed manuals were also available, both listed under RPO M20. A wide-ratio M20 with a 2.54:1 first gear was offered only for the two lower-powered 327s, while a close-ratio version with 2.20:1 low could be mated to the higher-output L76 and L84 small-blocks. Later in the year, the Borg-Warner box was traded for a Muncie four-speed, itself also built in close- and

wide-ratio forms, with the Muncie wide-ratio having a 2.56:1 first gear. Price for RPO M20, Borg-Warner or Muncie, close ratio or wide, was $188.30.

Additional performance options included an off-road exhaust system (N11)—which was officially offered but probably didn't appear until 1964—and sintered-metallic brakes (J65), priced at $37.70. Along with the metallic linings, RPO J65 also added finned drums, both

Obviously intended to go directly to the track, the Z06 Sting Ray represented the top of the heap in Corvette performance for 1963. Available only for coupes, RPO Z06 included the 360hp fuel-injected 327, special heavy-duty brakes and suspension, and a Positraction differential. Early paperwork also listed the large 36.5gal fuel tank and cast-aluminum knock-off wheels, but both were quickly dropped from the package. While the big tank remained as a separate option, RPO N03, the wheels never made production due to casting defects that led to air leaks.

It was called "the birdcage," and its welded steel structure is what held the Sting Ray's fiberglass shell together firmly. Weighing nearly twice as much as the steel reinforcement found beneath a 1962 Corvette convertible's skin, the birdcage meant less fiberglass could be used—the pounds gained by the steel frame was more than offset by a much lighter body, which was also stronger thanks to its additional reinforcement.

features going a long way toward reducing brake fade, a constant complaint lodged against Corvette binders. Comfort and convenience features on the options list included power windows (A31), Soft Ray tinted glass (A02, windshield; A01, all glass), the $236.75 removable hardtop for convertibles (C07), a woodgrain plastic

steering wheel (N34, introduced midyear), leather seats (priced at $80.70), signal-seeking Wonderbar AM radio (U65), an AM/FM radio (U69), and air conditioning (C60). Like power brakes and steering, air conditioning was offered as a Corvette option for the first time in 1963, although few apparently noticed—only 278 Sting Rays were equipped with air.

For Sting Ray buyers who couldn't care less about comfort and convenience, there was RPO Z06, the Special Performance Equipment group. A somewhat mysterious options package that went through various changes during its short, one-year run, RPO Z06 was clearly intended for one thing—and cruising the club wasn't it. Even if the first six 1963 Z06 Sting Ray coupes hadn't gone directly to

top race drivers in October 1962, it wouldn't have taken a rocket scientist to figure things out.

Obviously aimed at competition venues, RPO Z06 included an impressive lineup of heavy-duty speed parts. First and foremost was the 360hp fuel-injected 327 mated to a four-speed, the only powertrain combination available as part of the Special Performance package. A Positraction differential, special heavy-duty power brakes, heavy-duty suspension, an oversized 36.5gal fiberglass fuel tank, and five cast-aluminum knock-off wheels completed the deal, at least at first.

Most notable among that group was the brake system, beginning with the vacuum-assisted, dual-circuit master cylinder, a unit unique to the Z06 application. It was not the standard J50 power brake setup, as some have mistakenly concluded. Also contrary to common claims, the brakes themselves were not the J65 sintered-metallic pieces either. Z06 brake linings were sintered "cerametalix" and the shoes measured 11.75in long, compared to the J65's 11in shoes. And since engineers logically concluded that Z06 Sting Rays would spend most of their time on a track, where most drivers hopefully never used reverse, the automatic adjusting feature new to Corvette brakes for 1963 was modified to work with the car in forward motion, as opposed to the standard setup that was activated while backing up.

Like the J65 equipment, the Z06 cast-iron drums were finned for cooling, but efforts were made to help dissipate heat even further. Z06 backing plates were vented with screened openings allowing cooling air to enter the drum, where a fan mounted on the wheel hub helped keep the flow going. Rubber scoops, affectionately known as "elephant's ears," were attached to the backing plates to direct cool breezes into the fire. A Corvette performance option that dated back to 1957, elephant ears were delivered in a box inside a new 1963 Z06 Sting Ray, along with instructions on how to make the installation.

Heavy-duty Z06 suspension components included stiffer shocks, beefier springs, and a thick 0.94in front stabilizer bar. The attractive, aluminum knock-off rims—reportedly the result of Corvette racer and Gulf Oil executive Grady Davis' request for a quick-change road-racing wheel—measured 15x6in and included a special hub adapter that allowed attachment by a single three-pronged, threaded spinner (early prototypes used a two-eared spinner) in place of the typical five lugs.

Soon to be all the rage among the Corvette elite, the distinctive knock-offs (RPO P48) proved troublesome to produce early on and couldn't hold a tire seal. Dealers were forced to turn down requests for the $322.80 option and controversy still exists concerning how many 1963 Corvettes rolled off the lot with factory-installed P48 wheels. It is known that roughly a dozen pilot installations were attempted in St. Louis, but a regular-production example sold to the public has yet to be documented.

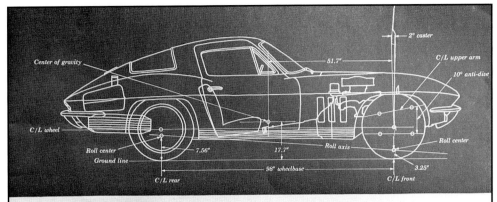

This kind of design gives Corvette surefooted handling characteristics.

I.R.S., unsprung weight and you

Some cars handle hard-traveling like your grandmother dispatching a garden snake with a rake. Lots of flailing and not much efficiency. That's because their suspensions were made for ordinary driving. But Corvette is no ordinary car. You expect it to have super handling, which is the reason for Corvette's surefooted independent rear suspension (I.R.S.)

There's nothing mystical about it. It all depends on those laws about mass and motion and suchlike. For instance, most cars have a conventional rear axle. It's sturdy, simple and serves admirably for regular passenger cars. But when there's a bump, both wheels and the differential react together because they are a single mass. The high inertia involved makes it unsatisfactory for a maximum performance machine.

Corvette's differential is bolted to the frame independent of the wheels so it doesn't have to go up and down when the wheels do. This lowers the inertia and lets the wheels react quickly, which keeps the tires planted more solidly. That's called lowering the unsprung weight ratio. The Corvette suspension also allows each wheel to react to the road without affecting the other and with minimum camber change of its own so each tire maintains a firm grip.

Mount all this on variable-rate springs front and rear, add ten degrees anti-dive geometry and a very low roll center at the front, give it Corvette's carefully calculated rearward weight bias and you've got a machine that's really tidy in a hard corner. Which is one reason Corvette is still America's only true production sports car.

Handling—The Chevrolet Way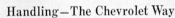

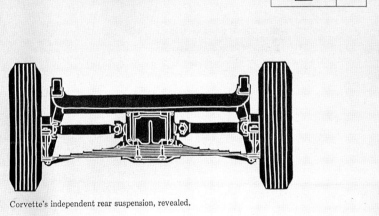

Corvette's independent rear suspension, revealed.

No, not that IRS; this acronym referred to the Sting Ray's innovative independent rear suspension, a design that helped cut unsprung weight in back by 33 percent. Save for springing, the

Corvette's IRS setup was basically a copy of the design used three years before on Duntov's CERV I experimental open-wheeled racer.

As it was, both the P48 wheels and oversized fuel tank were dropped from the Z06 lineup in December 1962 in a move to bring the option's initial hefty asking price of $1,818.14—almost half of the 1963 Corvette's base sticker—down to a more palatable $1,295. Adjusting the lineup also served to make the Z06 Sting Ray more attractive to brave nonracers who wanted to drive it on the street, as they then weren't forced to trade luggage space for the big fiberglass tank that had

Not all successful Corvette racers built in 1963 were high-profile Z06 models. This coupe was originally equipped with a 340hp 327 and saw regular street service until its original owner decided to put it to work on autocross circuits and in hillclimbs in Washington and Oregon beginning in 1965. Five years later, he went one step further, entering the car in SCCA B/Production competition. Today, this independent competition veteran is still proving itself in vintage racing events.

Right
Even though Chevrolet prognosticators had predicted the new Sting Ray coupe would dominate 1963 production, convertible sales picked up considerably late in the year, and the topless cars eventually overtook their closed counterparts. Total convertible production for 1963 was 10,919. Base price was $4,037. An optional removable hardtop, RPO C07, was also available and could be ordered at no extra cost if the folding top mechanism was deleted. Ordering RPO C07 with the folding top meant a buyer had to fork over an additional $236.75. In all, 5,739 Corvette convertible customers checked off RPO C07, including 1,099 who simply traded the soft top for the clamp-down roof. Original rubber in this case has long since been replaced by modern radials. Standard tires for 1963 were 6.70x15in four-ply rayon blackwalls. Two 6.70x15in tires were available at extra cost: the $15.70 P91 four-ply nylon blackwall and the $31.85 P92 four-ply rayon whitewall. P92 production dominated at 19,877 sets sold.

This prototype photo shows the 1963 Corvette's base Saginaw three-speed manual transmission. Among other things, the shift rod layout differed in regular production. Although originally listed behind all Sting Ray powerplants for 1963, the undesirable three-speed box was later dropped from the availability list for the top two performance powerplants early in 1964 production.

previously intruded into the cockpit area. Although no longer included as part of the Special Performance package, the 36.5gal tank could still be ordered by Z06 customers and standard Sting Ray fans alike since it remained available (for coupes only) as RPO N03, priced at a somewhat hefty $202.30. Incomplete factory records (actual production undoubtedly was higher) show sales of sixty-three N03 big tanks, both for competition purposes and some obvious nonracing applications where owners simply wanted extended range for long trips.

Another December 1962 change in the Z06 package involved model availability. Originally offered only with Model 837 coupes, RPO Z06 was also officially listed as an option for Model 867 convertibles for the first time in a distribution bulletin dated December 14. Although rumors of one Z06 convertible have floated about for years, no record of such a mating exists. Total Z06 coupe production was 199, with probably less than half of those surviving today as highly valued examples of just how hot a Corvette could get in 1963.

Even in standard trim, the 1963 Sting Ray was no slouch when it came to turning heads, either in motion or while standing still. Requests for the all-new models, *any* model, quickly swamped dealers in the fall of 1962 as soon as word got around.

"For the first time in its 10-year history," wrote *Motor Trend*'s Jim Wright, "the Corvette is in such demand that the factory has had to put on a second shift and still can't begin to supply cars fast enough. The waiting period is at least 60 days, and dealers won't 'deal' a bit on either coupes or roadsters. Both are going for the full sticker price, with absolutely no discount and very little (if any) over-allowance on trade-ins." Total Corvette production for 1963 topped 20,000 for the first time, with a near equal balance between the two bodystyles. After coupes started off the year as the hot ticket, convertible sales later caught up and passed them. In the end, coupes numbered 10,594, convertibles 10,919.

Driving a coupe or convertible, *Car Life*'s staff was so impressed with the Sting Ray, they awarded it their Award for Engi-

neering Excellence based on the fact that the Corvette had finally "achieved the refinement needed to match its great brute strength." Continued *Car Life*'s report, "the Sting Ray represents leadership in automotive design. It is tomorrow's car, on the street today."

Road & Track's curbside critics were especially fond of the Sting Ray's IRS advantage, especially compared to what came before. "The tendency for the [earlier Corvette's] rear wheels to spin freely on acceleration and for the rear end to come sliding around rather quickly during hard cornering was always there. Chevrolet engineers had done a good job with what they had at hand, but there just wasn't enough with which to work. That production-component live rear axle could hop and dance like an Apache with a hot foot." Three years after they had last tested a Corvette, *Road & Track*'s staff couldn't say enough about the way the redesigned 1963 model handled the road. "In a word, the new Sting Ray sticks! Whether you slam the car through an S-bend at 85 or pop the clutch at 5000rpm at the drag strip, the result is the same—great gripping gobs of traction."

Car Life's editors couldn't agree more. "Tricky, twisting roads are this Corvette's meat," read their December 1962 report. "With its new suspension it seems to lock onto them, going precisely where directed and sticking to the tightest corners without the shadow of a doubt. Where the old Corvette had an annoying penchant for swapping ends when cornered vigorously, the new one just sticks and storms. This suspension is the best thing since gumdrops!"

Jim Wright liked the way the Sting Ray stopped, once the sintered-metallic linings were in place and working. Explaining that "the car really deserves" discs, Wright at first pointed out that the standard drums were a bit lacking. "Sintered iron brake linings are optional and will certainly be found necessary for anyone planning to race, as fade is easily provoked with the standard linings, although the cooling-off period required to restore full efficiency is very short." As for the J65 brakes, "it's true that they require more pedal pressure to operate and are a trifle noisy on cold mornings," continued Wright, "but once they get warmed up they're excellent. The brakes in our test car pulled the Sting Ray down to quick straight-line stops time and again without any sudden locking of the wheels and without apparent fade. Several stretches of mountain roads showed that they could stand up to prolonged hard use without failure."

Hot Rod's Ray Brock was impressed by the 1963 Corvette's polite side. In his opinion, the newly offered optional "power steering should help immeasurably in increasing sales (as if they need it this year) because we've often heard ladies of all ages express a liking for Corvette styling and size but a dislike for the steering effort required to drive one daily." Proving that political correctness is a relatively recent phenomenon, Brock then concluded that "gals of all ages can also enjoy a Corvette thanks to power steering, power brakes and other accessories."

Drivers overseas could enjoy the car as well. Both *Autosport* and *The Motor* were treated to England's first encounters with the greatest American sports car yet to come down the pike. According to *Autosport*'s Patrick McNally in an early 1964 review, the 1963 Sting Ray coupe was a bloody winner: "Performance in a straight line is tremendous, the appearance not displeasing and the effect on the fair sex rewarding." "In most respects," reported *The Motor* in December 1963, "the Chevrolet Corvette Sting Ray is the equal of any G.T. car to be found on either side of the Atlantic." These comments seemed to prove *Car and Driver*'s claim that "at long last America has a formidable weapon to challenge Europe's fastest grand touring cars on their home ground."

Complaints, though minor relative to all the raves, were present and accounted for. *Car Life*'s crew didn't exactly like the prospect of wrestling heavy luggage into the "adequate-sized" storage area by way of the passenger compartment (since there was no rear deck lid, as there had been in 1962), nor were they thrilled by the hideaway headlights, calling them "a little too fussy for such an elegantly functional car." Fussy or not, those headlights didn't stop *Car Life* from enthusiastically labeling the 1963 Sting Ray "the best Corvette yet!"

Pointing to the typically imperfect fiberglass finish, Wright felt that "for a car that sells in the $4500–6000 range, [the Sting Ray] doesn't reflect the degree of quality control we feel it should." Continued his May 1963 *Motor Trend* report, "there still seems to be some difficulty in manufacturing a really smooth fiberglass body. While this isn't too apparent in a light-colored car, it becomes all too noticeable in some of the darker ones. When the light hits these from almost any angle, there's a definite rippled effect."

Such disappointments paled, however, in comparison to the runaway number one negative response, a complaint made by practically every automotive journalist who dared tried to look over his shoulder while at the 1963 Sting Ray's wheel. As much as he undoubtedly hated to admit it, Bill Mitchell was wrong; Duntov was right: the rear window "stinger" had to go. Although all magazines wholeheartedly agreed with Duntov, it was perhaps *Hop-Up*'s Ed Phillips who put the split-window situation in its proper perspective. "Visibility from the rearview mirror isn't too good," he wrote in a September 1963 review. "Chances are you'd probably *hear* a motorcycle cop on your tail before you could see him."

Why would a motorcycle cop be on a Sting Ray's tail? While *Car Life*'s test of a 300hp L75 Corvette coupe equipped with the optional Powerglide automatic produced an average quarter-mile time of 15.5sec at 86mph, *Motor Trend* demonstrated what the top-of-the-heap 360hp fuelie could do for straight-line performance. With a close-ratio four-speed and a 3.70:1 Positraction rear end, *Motor Trend*'s L84 Sting Ray coupe tripped the lights in 14.5sec, topping out at 102mph. Sixty miles per hour from rest took but 5.8sec, while top speed was listed as 130mph. With that kind of power, who needed to look behind anyway?

As for Z06 performance, that was proven on the track at Riverside on October 13, 1962, when Doug Hooper's Sting Ray bested a Porsche to win the *Los Angeles Times* Three-Hour Invitational. It was a win, sure, but Duntov didn't exactly feel like celebrating after watching another production racer launch its career that

Offered only for the base 250hp 327 and the 300hp L75, the M35 Powerglide automatic transmission is shown here in a 1963 prototype installation. Missing in this photo are the two oil cooler lines that normally ran from the Powerglide case's right side near where the dipstick tube appears from behind the transmission's ribbed center section.

day. After Carroll Shelby's 1962 proposal to build a few rebodied, lightweight Corvettes had been rejected by Chevrolet, he turned to Dearborn as a power source for an exciting Anglo-American hybrid machine. With a warmed-over Ford Windsor V-8 beneath its British-built aluminum skin, Shelby's AC Cobra was easily the Z06's match, and perhaps only a Cobra breakdown saved the four-car Corvette team from a discouraging defeat during both sports cars' Riverside debut. That debut was only the beginning for the Cobra-Corvette wars.

Long a dominant force in SCCA competition, Chevrolet's Sting Ray would end up being bumped out of the 1964 A-Production championship by Shelby-American's Ford-based Cobra, and it would be five years before another Corvette would make its way back to the top. But Duntov had been considering a more competitive Corvette even before the Cobra had entered the scene. Based on the all-new 1963 Sting Ray, Zora's lightweight racer would be everything his '57 Super Sport had been and much more. The car would be a "Grand Sport."

Chapter Three

Heirs to the Throne

Duntov's Ill-Fated Grand Sports

All five of them still exist, to the dismay of General Motors' officials who thirty years ago had demanded they be done away with. Corvette Grand Sports—three coupes and two roadsters—when first conceived in the summer of 1962, these burly, lightweight, all-out racing machines represented the best Zora Duntov could offer as far as world-class, Federation Internationale de l'Automobile (FIA) sanctioned Grand Touring competition was concerned. Problem was, Chevrolet—like all of Detroit—wasn't supposed to be involved in racing, on this country's tracks or any other's; the Automobile Manufacturers Association's so-called ban on factory-supported competition had seen to that in June 1957. But ban be damned, Duntov powered up his Grand Sport project five years later, with enthusiastic backing from Chevrolet general manager Semon "Bunkie" Knudsen, only to have the plug pulled once GM's top brass decided enough was enough. In January 1963 the order came down from the fourteenth floor to end such politically incorrect shenanigans, effectively concluding the Grand Sport story before it could be written.

Nonetheless, various chapters did follow as the five Grand Sports built before GM's ax fell rolled out Chevrolet Engineering's back door into a succession of racers' hands, some supposedly independent, others definitely so. After that came an even longer line of collectors bent on preserving these high-priced pieces of Corvette racing history.

Through it all, the awesome Grand Sports have persevered, although all five have taken on differing identities over the years. Paint schemes varied with each succeeding racing team, bodywork was modified as scoops and flares were experimented with, and both small-block and big-block power was used. Once in the collector realm, a Grand Sport posed an interesting problem for restorers as "originality" in this case could be translated so many different ways. Unmistakable, however, is what the Grand Sports could have meant to Duntov's dreams of racing glory had the project been allowed to fully develop. Sure, the Grand Sports did race, but not while proudly waving the Chevrolet banner as Knudsen and Duntov had intended, nor in the optimum form originally planned.

In the end, the disappointing display was reminiscent of the Corvette Super Sport debacle in 1957. After heat dissipation difficulties abruptly ended the car's competition debut at Sebring, the ensuing AMA anti-racing decree brought the entire project to a screaming halt. From there, any and all racing involvement by

Various modifications were made to the Grand Sports almost immediately after they hit the track in 1963 as demands of competition were met. Among these modifications was the addition of a huge hood scoop to aid engine cooling (as well as to clear the four sidedraft Weber carburetors underneath) and equally large fender flares, which were required to house wider wheels (8.5in fronts, 9.5in rears) and Firestone tires. A series of openings were also added across the tail to improve both brake and differential cooling.

Early Grand Sport plans called for an unconventional 377ci alloy small-block with special heads featuring two spark plugs per cylinder, but that powerplant never saw an engine bay. This more conventional 377ci aluminum small-block, with its four Weber two-barrel carburetors, did make it under the Grand Sport's hood. In 1963, this engine was reported to produce 485hp at 6000rpm, more than ample power as ably demonstrated during Nassau Speed Week that year. Dave Friedman photo

the Corvette engineering crew was completely covert, with much unauthorized, underground support going to Dr. Dick Thompson's supposedly independent efforts on the SCCA circuit.

Duntov tried again in 1959, creating the enigmatic CERV I. Although early discussions did mention possible appearances at Pikes Peak and Indianapolis, GM management, still sticking tight to the AMA ban, wouldn't have anything of it, instead making it quite clear the CERV I

was intended for nothing more than tire and suspension testing. But Duntov wanted a full-blooded racing Corvette, not a test track queen, and he wouldn't be denied.

The arrival of both Bunkie Knudsen in November 1961 and the all-new regular-production Sting Ray in late 1962 represented major stepping stones toward Duntov's next attempt to put his Corvette on the international racing map. With its improved chassis, the 1963 Sting Ray ob-

Shown here is the Grand Sport's rigid, tube frame and large 36.5gal gas tank. Notice the conventional 360hp fuel-injected 327 originally installed in lieu of the larger, more exotic small-block initially planned for the Grand Sport. Grand Sports also initially rolled on relatively

skinny Halibrand knock-off wheels wearing equally skinny rubber—all that changed once the cars got a taste of the track. Unlike a standard 1963 Sting Ray, a Grand Sport featured a rear deck lid to supply access to that spare tire.

Semon E. "Bunkie" Knudsen had joined Pontiac in 1956 as GM's youngest ever divisional general manager and then successfully turned Pontiac's image around, thanks to a heavy dose of performance and youthful design pizzazz. Always a big fan of high performance, Knudsen was just the man Duntov needed at the top when Bunkie moved over to Chevrolet in November 1961. It was Knudsen's enthusiastic support that helped Zora Duntov kick off his Grand Sport project. But Knudsen didn't make all the decisions, and GM's anti-racing edict of January 1963 brought an abrupt end to Duntov's project. Knudsen later jumped GM's ship in 1968 and tried the same high-powered practices at Ford before he was abruptly fired by Henry Ford II some eighteen months later.

viously offered distinct advantages for building a production-based racing version. Weight remained a problem, however, even though Duntov had hoped the all-new Corvette coupe would end up considerably lighter than its forerunners.

As for Knudsen, his reputation as an avid performance promoter was well established before he slipped into Chevrolet's general manager shoes. As Pontiac's chief from 1956 to 1961, Knudsen had been the driving force behind the once-stagnant division's newfound youthful image, an image that wasn't hurt in the least by Pontiac Motor Division's growing dominance of the early 1960s NASCAR stock car scene. Clearly, Bunkie and Zora thought a lot alike, especially concerning the value of victories at the track relating to future developments. Wrote *Car and Driver's* Jan Norbye, "with a genuine sports car on his hands, and an attitude several degrees off perfect alignment with the AMA resolution, [Knudsen] may find the means of letting Duntov take up where he left off in 1957. Surely this would be the logical thing, for nobody at

Chevrolet Engineering, least of all Zora Arkus-Duntov, allows himself to forget that they have to have a still better Corvette ten years from now."

But what of the infamous AMA anti-racing resolution? Obviously Pontiac's performance developments under Knudsen's directions were contrary to the 1957 edict, and Ford and Chrysler had already begun showing little regard for the ban a few years before Bunkie joined Chevrolet. Then, in June 1962, Henry Ford II issued a press release announcing his company's plans to ignore the AMA directive and actively pursue racing successes. The 300-word release mentioned how Dearborn initially adhered "to the spirit and letter of the recommendations." However, the release continued, "as time passed, some car divisions [Pontiac, perhaps?] interpreted the resolution more and more freely, with the result that increasing emphasis was placed on speed, horsepower, and racing. As a result, Ford Motor Company feels that the resolution has come to have neither purpose nor effect. Accordingly, we have notified [the AMA] that we feel

we can better establish our own standards of conduct with respect to the manner in which the performance of our vehicles is to be promoted and advertised."

Chrysler issued a similar statement soon after, helping kick off a fierce four-year battle between two of Detroit's Big Three on NASCAR's superspeedways. At the same time, Dearborn's Total Performance campaign was marching toward glorious victory at Le Mans, where on June 19, 1966, Ford Motor Company became the first American auto maker to win France's legendary 24 Hours classic as three Ford-powered GT-40s convincingly crossed the finish in succession. It was the glory Duntov had long sought, and it was the satisfaction he would be continually denied.

In 1960, Duntov and a few of his men had assisted racing tycoon Briggs Cunningham in his attempt to field a three-Corvette team for Le Mans. Along with another 1960 Corvette, Cunning-

Although Zora Duntov initially planned to build 125 Corvette Grand Sport racers, only five were unleashed late in 1962 before GM officials squelched the project. Featuring a tube frame and an especially lightweight, one-piece fiberglass shell, a Grand Sport coupe weighed in at roughly 1,000 pounds less than its regular-production Sting Ray counterpart. This is Grand Sport number 005, owned by NASCAR engine builder and Corvette collector Bill Tower of Plant City, Florida. Grand Sport coupe numbers 001 and 002 were converted into roadsters in 1964 in an attempt to improve aerodynamics.

ham's three cars impressed the Europeans with their power and appearance, but various mishaps limited their performance. Bad breaks aside, one of the Cunningham Corvettes, driven by John Fitch and Bob Grossman, did manage a respectable eighth-place overall finish, high enough to rank as one of the greatest track achievements to date for Chevrolet's fiberglass two-seater. Zora, however, still wanted more. Much more.

After briefly toying with the possibilities of taking the CERV I ideal to the track, Duntov began considering plan B. Greatly influencing his next competition approach was a 1962 FIA announcement detailing a restructuring of its World Manufacturers Championship rules. In 1963, Grand Touring cars would be eligible for that championship as long as a manufacturer "homologated" (legalized) its GT

entry by building at least 100 "regular-production" examples in a given twelve-month period. Also announced was the intriguing fact that no upper displacement limit would be put on these GT competitors, a point not lost on either Duntov or Carroll Shelby. Both were immediately at work on rival GT projects; Duntov, of course, for Chevrolet, Shelby for Ford.

With Chevrolet's performance-minded Knudsen now at the top running interference for him, Zora felt confident enough in 1962 to attempt an all-out GT racing project, with or without upper office approval. He would use the new Sting Ray as a base, although a lot of unnecessary, speed-robbing weight would have to be trimmed before a suitable racing version could emerge at a competitive level. Simply referred to as the "light-

weight Corvette" early on, that racing Sting Ray would become the Grand Sport.

Duntov's engineers kicked off the Grand Sport project in the summer of 1962 with a tubular-steel frame modeled after the standard Sting Ray's ladder-type design on an identical wheelbase (98in) with narrowed, parallel tubes instead of wide perimeter rails. Both lighter and stronger at the same time, the Grand Sport's purpose-built frame reportedly weighed ninety-four pounds less than its regular-production counterpart, and it also incorporated mounting points for a full roll cage. Equally light was the aluminum alloy differential housing used in back. With its transverse leaf spring and three-link arrangement, the Grand Sport's IRS design was certainly familiar, but differences between these pieces and stock

In 1957, Duntov's first attempt at international racing glory failed somewhat miserably as his purpose-built Super Sport succumbed early to overheating problems at Sebring. Five years later he was ready to try again with another purpose-built Corvette, a car that looked like its regular-production counterparts but was considerably modified beneath the skin.

Below
Specially hand-laid to paper-thin specifications (0.040in) with an eye towards keeping weight down, the Grand Sport's fiberglass body was also "trimmed down" here and there to improve aerodynamics. Among other things, the roof is narrower and the windshield raked back farther compared to a standard 1963 Corvette. Owner Bill Tower calls the Grand Sport "a 7/8ths model of the stock Sting Ray." Notice the exposed fitting on the front fender (directly behind Bill Scott's name); its tied to a hydraulic jacking system installed to expedite pit shops.

The Grand Sport's greatest days in the sun came in the Bahamas in December 1963 during Nassau Speed Week. Three Cadillac Blue Grand Sports, chassis numbers 003, 004, and 005, showed up under the Mecom Racing Team banner to put Carroll Shelby and his Cobras in their place. Along with the Grand Sports, wealthy Texan John Mecom also brought along a Lola-Chevrolet, a Cooper-Chevrolet, a Scarab, and the Zerex-Cooper Special. Mecom drivers included Roger Penske, A. J. Foyt, Jim Hall, Dr. Dick Thompson, and Augie Pabst. Shown here is Penske in Grand Sport 004 (car number 50 at lower left) leading the pack at Nassau during practice laps. Pabst's Chevy-Lola, car number 00, is directly behind Penske, followed by Thompson in GS 005 (car number 80) and Hall driving Grand Sport 003. Although none of the Grand Sports finished first in the three races held that week, they did beat the Ford-powered Cobras at every turn, which in itself was enough of a victory in Duntov's eyes. Dave Friedman photo

parts were like night and day. Beefed throughout, the Grand Sport IRS layout also helped trim the fat with modified sheet-steel trailing-arm hub carriers drilled for reduced weight.

Contributing as well to the Grand Sport's diet was an aluminum steering box, special front suspension A-arms welded up from sheet steel, and a set of 15x6in Halibrand magnesium knock-off wheels. Each wheel tipped the scales at only 16.5lb. Solid 11.75in Girling discs with three-piston calipers were mounted at all four corners, while heavy-duty front coil springs, various hardened, reinforced steering pieces, and stiff Delco shocks completed the chassis.

Atop that chassis went a special one-piece fiberglass shell laid up by hand with super-thin panels for additional lightness.

Certain measurements here and there—such as slightly more windshield slope and a lower, narrowed roofline—differed from stock standards as Duntov's designers attempted to improve, however minimally, on the new Sting Ray's less-than-desirable high-speed aerodynamics. Relative to entrenched European rivals, Chevrolet's 1963 Corvette was still a veritable brick in the wind even though it looked so sleek and slippery. Although measurably smaller than typical American designs, Sting Ray frontal area remained considerable, from a competition perspective, and also contributed to the body's tendency to lift as speeds increased. It was this unwanted lift that plagued Grand Sports, as well as all racing Corvettes built from 1963 to 1967, throughout their abbreviated competition careers.

Additional differences between the stock Sting Ray shell and its flimsy Grand Sport copy included enlarged wheelhouses to allow the use of bigger tires, a rear deck lid for spare tire access, and fixed headlights mounted behind clear plexiglass in place of the heavy hideaway units. Even more weight was trimmed by using plexiglass windows (the windshield remained glass) with hand lifts instead of regulators, while aluminum underbody reinforcement did the job normally performed by the Sting Ray's steel birdcage. In back, Mitchell's pesky stinger window partition was not included for obvious reasons, and a fuel filler for the 36.5gal fiberglass gas tank protruded from the roof behind the passenger door.

Inside, a standard Sting Ray dash housed a typical collection of gauges, but most notable was the stock-looking speedometer that, on closer inspection, registered 200mph. Although the steering wheel appeared stock, it was actually modeled after the standard Sting Ray unit using a stainless steel three-spoke rim wrapped in teakwood. Certainly not stock was the exceptionally quick steering ratio requiring only two turns lock-to-lock. Untypically plush (for a race car) full carpeting and fiberglass bucket seats completed the package.

As for power, Duntov's initial plans called for an exotic all-aluminum small-block displacing 377ci. With four Weber 58mm IDA two-barrel carburetors, twin spark plugs in each combustion chamber, and headers, the 377ci Grand Sport V-8 reportedly made 550hp on the dyno, more than enough muscle, it was hoped, to overwhelm the car's disappointing aerodynamics. While awaiting its engine,

Following pages
In an attempt to improve the Grand Sport's wind-cheating abilities, the first two Grand Sport Coupes were transformed into roadsters in 1964. But before the idea could be proven on the track at Daytona, GM officials again ordered an end to the racing involvement they had supposedly canceled in January 1963. After sitting in storage for nearly two years, the two roadsters went to Roger Penske early in 1966. Penske let Grand Sport 002 go to George Wintersteen, who, like Penske, dropped in a 427 big-block and went racing. Penske's 427-powered 001 roadster debuted at Sebring in March 1966 but broke down after only three hours. Dave Friedman photo

With somewhat plush full carpeting, a stock-looking dash and a teakwood-rimmed steering wheel, the Grand Sport's interior appeared almost civilized, even though the car itself was a real beast. Notice the bulge in the driver's footwell where the tube frame member runs under the compartment floor. While a Grand Sport's main perimeter tubes ran parallel from front to back, a standard Sting Ray frame featured widely spaced perimeter rails that kicked out under the door sills to maximize passenger compartment floor space.

Hiding beneath those exotic 58mm Weber side-draft carburetors is an aluminum 377ci small-block, an all-out racing version of the 327 found under a standard 1963 Sting Ray's hood. The special intake was of cross-ram design, meaning the Webers on the right fed the heads on the left, while the Webers on the left fed the heads on the right.

Grand Sport number 001 was fitted with an aluminum version of the Sting Ray's fuel-injected 327 and readied for testing at Sebring in December 1962. It was the first of 125 lightweight Corvettes Duntov intended to build for GT competition, with homologation papers being filed with the FIA that same month. In those papers, the Grand Sport's weight was listed as 1,908lb, more than a half-ton less than the standard 1963 Sting Ray.

As Duntov stood poised to unleash his Grand Sports on the world, fate once again stepped in to cut him off at the knees. On January 21, 1963, GM chairman Frederick Donner and president John Gordon dropped their ax in the form of a memo informing all division heads to cancel certain performance projects then under way. Victims of Donner's ax included Pontiac's NASCAR-dominating Super Duty program and Chevrolet's Mark II Mystery Motor, itself a promising NASCAR weapon of the future. The Grand Sport, of course, was canceled as well.

One month later, Donner explained GM's apparent change of heart at a February 16 press conference. "Ever since the AMA adopted—I think you can term it a recommendation—back in 1957," he said, "we have had a policy on our books, and we haven't had any change in it." But how could Duntov have built the Grand Sport if GM truly had been adhering to the AMA recommendation? "Very often you run into interpretations of policies that to an outsider might look like violations—that distance between interpretation and violation is a very delicate one."

What these words smelled like wasn't delicate at all. Donner and Gordon's people obviously had looked the other way until outside pressures forced them to reign in what were perceived to be runaway performance practices. General Motors might have liked everyone to think it was responding to growing government concerns over automotive safety, but perhaps more close to the truth was GM's

This movie camera was installed by Chevrolet to investigate the Grand Sport's performance on the track, both visually and through audio pickup. The film not only allowed engineers see how the car made it through the turns, it also let them listen to engine sounds that indicated the driver's choice of shift points, both up and down.

Right
The Grand Sport's dash does appear stock at first glance, but closer inspection reveals the standard 160mph Sting Ray speedometer has been replaced by this more suitable 200mph unit.

concern over impending federal antitrust action. By putting a stop to Chevrolet and Pontiac's racing activities, GM officials succeeded in diverting any additional unwanted federal attention, in essence keeping their nose clean while they continued to tiptoe around what some legislators viewed as monopolistic business practices.

No matter how you sliced it, though, the end result remained a stillborn birth for Duntov's Grand Sport. The 377 aluminum engine never reached "regular" production, and only five GS chassis had been completed before the project was canceled.

Case closed?

Not at all. From there, the five Grand Sports managed to sneak out Chevrolet

Co-driven by Roger Penske and Jim Hall, Grand Sport 005 demonstrates the breed's propensity towards excessive nose lift at high speeds during the 12 Hours of Sebring in March 1964. On the way to finishing eighteenth overall, Penske nearly broke the Sebring lap record in GS 005, touring the 5.2-mile course in 3min 12.2sec, just short of John Surtees' 3min 11.4sec lap turned in a Ferrari two years before. Dave Friedman photo

Engineering's still-open "back door" and enter the racing world with much unauthorized support from Duntov and his engineers. Two of the cars were equipped with 360hp fuel-injected 327s and "loaned" to Chevrolet's racer "friends" Dick Doane and Gulf Oil executive Grady

Davis. Since they failed to meet standard production class requirements, the Grand Sports were considered prototypes, and thus ended up in SCCA's C-Modified class, where they ran—with little success—against unlimited racing machines like the Scarab and Chaparral, both also powered by Chevrolet V-8s.

Once the Grand Sport coupes were in the wild, they began sprouting various louvers, holes, and vents for added cooling, as well as spoilers and fender flares, while the transparent headlight shields were later replaced with covers. Early in 1964, a pneumatic jacking system was included to make pit stops easier and quicker. An imposing scoop was added to the

hood, wheels and tires grew massive, and different engines were tried, including the 427 Mark IV big-block in 1966. But most prominent among the long list of Grand Sport modifications made over the years was the conversion of chassis numbers 001 and 002 from coupes into roadsters.

By removing the roof and cutting down the windscreen, Duntov had hoped to cure the Grand Sport's aerodynamic difficulties, with the specific goal being to better the cars' chances during the Daytona Continental, to be held February 16, 1964. Along with the short windscreen, the Grand Sport roadsters also got a fiberglass-encased roll bar. Determining whether the roadster conversion im-

proved the Grand Sport's ability to cut the wind was delayed, however, as the two cars didn't make it to Florida, at least not in 1964.

GM killjoys stepped in once again, this time after reading the papers, where headlines like the New York *Herald Tribune*'s "Don't Look Now but That's a Chevy Tooling Up in the Pits" had them hopping mad. For a car that was supposed to be scrapped, the Grand Sport had been mysteriously active in 1963, including a wild foray to the Bahamas by an all-star racing team fielded by Texan John Mecom. Arriving November 30 on the docks for the Nassau Speed Weeks, the Mecom Racing Team showed up with a lot of factory support, three Grand Sports, and legendary drivers Roger Penske, Augie Pabst, Jim Hall, and A. J. Foyt. When the dust had cleared by week's end, the Grand Sports had thoroughly embarrassed Carroll Shelby's Cobras—and they had also drawn the ire of GM chiefs who thought they had put an end to such extracurricular affairs.

They then stepped in again, this time

hitting Bunkie Knudsen where it hurt, threatening him with his annual bonus unless he put a stop to the Grand Sport project once and for all. That he did; the three coupes were eventually sold off, as were the two freshly converted roadsters. From there, the three Grand Sport coupes went through various racers' hands, including those of John Mecom, Jim Hall, and Roger Penske. Penske also bought the two roadsters, dropping a 427 into one of them and taking it to Sebring in March 1966. All five cars continued to compete at various levels, with the last major appearance for a Grand Sport roadster (number 002) coming in June 1966 at Mosport in Ontario. A Grand Sport coupe (number 004) toured a big-time track (Daytona) for the last time in February 1967.

Although there were racing successes, the Grand Sport legacy certainly didn't develop the way Duntov had intended when he first envisioned his lightweight Corvette in 1962. But interference from the front office alone couldn't be blamed. At best, the Grand Sports were brutal

George Wintersteen at the wheel of Grand Sport 002 at Ontario's Mosport track in June 1966, the last major competition appearance for the GS roadsters. Wintersteen reportedly sold his Grand Sport soon afterward for $6,700. Dave Friedman photo

beasts, both advanced and crude at the same time. Even if Chevrolet had been allowed to produce all 125 cars, and fit them with that hot 377ci aluminum V-8, the lightweight Corvettes still would have represented old news almost overnight. By the mid-1960s, the world racing scene was changing rapidly, and as we all know today, technology waits for no one. As Dick Guldstrand later told *Automobile Quarterly*'s John Heilig, "the mid-engined trick cars started to show up around mid-1965, making the Grand Sports little more than plastic pachyderms."

Grand Sport performance, however, was by no means peanuts. Those lucky enough to have seen one of Duntov's lightweight Corvettes in action will never forget.

Chapter Four

1964

Split Decision

Sure, the 1963 Sting Ray was a great car, a veritable landmark in American automobile production history. Styling was sensational, mechanicals were state of the art (at least from a Yankee perspective), and all-around performance was as good as it got within these shores thirty years ago. But being a man-made machine, there were glitches, however minor. For the most part, complaints could be written off, considering that this was a sports car, and sports cars do have certain inherent deficiencies. Physical laws being the same in most states, there was only so much room to work with considering the Corvette's tight parameters, both literally and figuratively.

Typically, more room for legs would have meant less room for engine. More room for hats would have meant disruption of the classic lines Shinoda had pained over for so long. More room for seats would have upset the balance Duntov desired. OK, there wasn't a trunk lid and stowing heavy bags was a little tough through the passenger compartment, but at least there was ample storage. Just think, you could have had an MG!

Maybe the ride was a bit harsh for some—again, remember, this was a sports car; a big, brawny American sports car. Enough said. As for brakes, well, there was no excuse here except for the plain fact that American auto makers had yet to get serious about stopping power. In Corvette terms, a proper response was a year away. There was, however, one problem area that wouldn't wait another year for a solution. You had to be blind to miss it, for even if you had never seen a 1963 Sting Ray, you could have read all about it in any popular magazine.

"Our only complaint about the interior was in the coupe," explained *Road & Track*, "where all we could see in the rear view mirror was that silly bar splitting the rear window down the middle." According to *Car Life*, "the bar down the center of the rear window makes it all but impossible to see out via the rearview mirror." As *Motor Trend*'s Jim Wright saw it, "the rear window on the coupe is designed more for looks than practicality, and any decent view to the rear will have to be through an exterior side mirror." *Car and Driver* concluded that "luggage space is surprisingly roomy but [the] central window partition ruins rear view." Slings and arrows even came from overseas, with England's *Autosport* reporting that "nothing can be seen of the tail through the divided rear window, which makes reversing in confined quarters rather precarious."

Base price for a Corvette convertible was $4,037 in 1964. As in 1963, the standard convertible top color was black, with either beige or white available at no extra cost. Installed on 7,843 1964 convertibles, the white top was most popular that year, followed by black (4,721), and beige (591). Another 1,220 1964 Corvette convertibles were not equipped with soft tops as customers chose to opt for the C07 removable hardtop as a no-cost option. Again, when RPO C07 was ordered along with the folding top the removable hardtop became a $236.75 option.

Non-functional in 1963, the small roof vents behind the Sting Ray coupes door were brought to life in 1964, at least on the driver's side. Used in both 1964 and 1965, this standard electric ventilation system used those vents to exhaust interior air. The idea worked much better on paper than in real life.

Even Bill Mitchell was quick to admit that the original Sting Ray's split-window layout, the pet theme he had battled Duntov for, was indeed a hazard. Not long after the all-new 1963 Corvette coupe had hit the streets, buyers were al-

ready cutting out Mitchell's stinger, replacing the two curved glass panes with one solid piece of plexiglass. Of course, that was a trend later reversed once the split-window Sting Rays started gaining considerable value as collectible classics. But who could have known thirty years ago?

On the other hand, predicting in 1963 what would happen to the Corvette body one year down the road was a stone-cold cinch in everyone's eyes. Rolling out in basically identical form, Chevrolet's second-edition Sting Ray de-

buted sans stinger in the fall of 1963, much to the delight of drivers who preferred seeing what they were about to back over. Describing the next great Corvette as "docile but no fossil, and agile but not fragile," *Road & Track*'s reviewers pointed out the obvious in their March 1964 report. "The body design of the 1964 Sting Ray remains little changed from 1963," they wrote, "although we were pleased to note that the central division in the rear window has been eliminated, with a consequent improvement in vision."

Other exterior changes were minor, with typically restyled wheel covers representing the most noticeable new feature. Harder to spot were the revamped rocker moldings with only three black-painted horizontal indentations instead of eight. Responding to barbs aimed at various unnecessary, nonfunctional trim tricks, Mitchell's crew removed the two dummy grilles in the hood, however, cost-awareness resulted in a return of the two hood depressions where the grilles had resided in 1963. Equally purposeless the year before, the 1963 coupe's so-called air outlets behind the doors were restyled and made functional, at least on the driver's side, where an electric ventilation motor, located in cramped quarters behind the left rear wheelwell, tried somewhat vainly to push out the 1964 Sting Ray's bad air. A nice idea, but it was severely limited by the small, three-speed motor's weak lungs. The equipment was deleted after 1965.

Remaining welcomed advancements came beneath the skin and addressed certain customer complaints concerning a gremlin Detroit's acronym artists like to call "NVH"—noise, vibration, and harshness. After determining that the 1963 frame had transmitted too much road noise inside the body, Duntov's engineers upgraded the body mounts (modifications varied from coupe to convertible) for 1964 using "rubber biscuit" insulators. New cotton-fiber insulation was added below the carpet and a foil-backed "insulation blanket" went on the firewall in the engine compartment. Stiffened fiberglass bodywork in back also helped reduce resonation, a common problem with GRP (glass-reinforced plastic) construction.

Other NVH attacks were turned back inside, where the shifter's annoying buzzing was cured with a new rubber boot and rubber linkage bushings. Underneath, noise and vibration were minimized by revising muffler internals and adding a more flexible tailpipe hanger also made of rubber. Additionally, front exhaust system mounts were moved from the frame cross-member to the transmission mounting hardware, further cutting pesky vibrations.

As for harshness, an already relatively "soft" ride (from a performance perspective) was softened even more by adding variable-rate springs and recalibrated

Chevrolet's excellent aluminum-case Muncie four-speed, RPO M20, was nearly identical to the Muncie gearbox that had debuted midyear in 1963 save for the shift rods, which were beefier in 1964. Price for the 1964 M20 box, wide- or close-ratio, was $188.30.

shocks. Wound tighter at the top than bottom, the front coil springs "relaxed" during normal operation, yet firmed-up when compressed. A similar variable-rate effect was created in back by forming the downward-curved transverse spring's shorter leaves with less curvature, meaning they would only add more stiffness to the spring as a whole under heavy compression. Overall, the 1964 Corvette's standard suspension easily represented America's best compromise between all-out road-hugging performance and pleasant boulevard-bound comfort.

"By using relatively soft (for sports cars) springing and firm damping," reported *Car Life*, "the Sting Ray avoids the choppiness expected from such a short wheelbase." *Road & Track*'s test drivers agreed, claiming "the suspension is stiffer than we expected but not uncomfortable and does a good job on very bad road surfaces. It is helped considerably by a weight distribution [with] a slight rearward bias and this distribution has also

done a lot for steering to the extent that we feel it makes power steering unnecessary under most circumstances."

Car Life's lead-foot journalists also liked how Duntov's soft-spoken suspension let its presence be known when angered. "Full-throttle acceleration from rest caused the car to hunker down and leap off, with only minimum wheelspin." Again, *Road & Track* was right there to back up *Car Life*'s bragging: "The Sting Ray tended to squat down on its rear suspension when leaving the line, with never so much as a chirp from its tires, and then gobble up the strip." It certainly appeared as if the 1964 Corvette had all bases pretty well covered.

Along with reducing NVH, Mitchell, Duntov, and the boys also paid closer attention to quality control during body construction, which, beginning late in 1963, was split between the St. Louis assembly plant and Dow Smith, a division of the A. O. Smith Company in Livonia,
continued on page 65

One Step Backward

XP-819—CHEVROLET'S REAR-ENGINED CORVETTE PROTOTYPE

General Motors' long, seemingly endless line of Corvette prototypes, competition machines, and show cars has featured more than its fair share of legendary vehicles, some more notable than others.

Credited to Chevrolet engineer Frank Winchell, the rear-engined XP-819 was built in 1964 and foretold much of the new Corvette look that would debut for 1968—which was no coincidence since the body was designed by Larry Shinoda, the same man who created both the 1963 Sting Ray and 1968 Corvette restyle. XP-819's body-colored urethane front bumper and lift-off one-piece top (removed in this photo) were also signs of things to come. Overall height was only 44in.

Having essentially rolled right off a GM Motorama stage itself in January 1953, Chevrolet's first-edition Corvette served as the base in 1954 for three more Motorama dream cars: a hardtop version, the fastback Corvair, and the Nomad sport wagon, the last model serving as inspiration for the regular-production passenger-line Nomads of 1955–1957. Three innovative racing Corvettes, the production-based SR-2, the tube-frame Super Sport, and the sleek Stingray, hit the track in 1956, 1957, and 1959, respectively. One year later, Bill Mitchell's futuristic, duck-tailed XP-700 appeared, tipping off the 1961 Corvette's rear-end restyle.

More renowned are GM's two engineering experiments—CERV (Chevrolet Experimental Research Vehicle) I and II—and the intimidating Grand Sport racers. CERV I was built in 1959 and helped lay the groundwork for the 1963 Sting Ray's standard independent rear suspension, while the 427-powered, all-wheel-drive CERV II emerged in 1963. Duntov's brutal Grand Sports were initially conceived in late 1962 as all-out responses to Carroll Shelby's Ford-powered Cobras, with only five produced before corporate anti-racing pressures nipped the project in the bud.

Recognizable Corvette styling studies included Larry Shinoda's XP-755 Shark (later the Mako Shark I) of 1961 and the Mako Shark II of 1965, originally a nonfunctional mockup that later reappeared in running form as the Manta Ray in 1969. Between the Mako Shark II and Manta Ray came the unconventional

Astro I with its mid-engined layout, an idea introduced earlier by the CERV vehicles and probably best demonstrated in the form of the aluminum-bodied XP-895 (a steel shell version was also built) in 1972. Even more unconventional were two mid-engined prototypes un-

veiled in 1973 using Wankel rotary power.

But as intriguing as the various experimental, or "XP," Corvettes have been over the years, not all made it into the show circuit limelight. Perhaps most prominent among the forgotten proto-

The XP-819's Kamm-backed tail hinged upward, exposing a small-block V-8 perched backward off a Pontiac automatic transaxle, while the nose section tilted up as well—in a fashion similar to today's Corvettes—to allow access to the battery and radiator. A small storage compartment—accessed through an exterior deck lid—was incorporated behind the seats.

Some parts, such as the inner door knobs, were right off the standard Sting Ray parts shelf, but nearly everything else seen here was custom fabricated for the XP-819, including the shoulder harnesses and exotic bucket seats. Seats were fixed, meaning the footpedals had to be adjustable—in this case electrically—to meet varying driver reaches. The small lever just ahead of the seatbelt perches on the front of the console is the automatic transaxle shifter, while the electric pedal adjust-ment switches are in between those perches. A particularly unique feature of the XP-819 prototype was its form-fitting inner door panels which when closed made up the outside bolsters for the deeply recessed, somewhat cramped bucket seats. Notice the small, black stick-on label just to the left of the gauges at the top of the dash. It reads "DEV. CAR—SEE NIES," a reference to engineer Larry Nies, who designed the backbone-type chassis for this odd developmental machine.

types was XP-819, a radical rear-engined Corvette that came and went in 1964 before anyone outside GM's inner circle had a chance to even raise an eyebrow, let alone debate its merits, or lack thereof. Thirteen years later, XP-819 mysteriously returned from apparent oblivion to take its place among the show field at the annual Bloomington Gold Corvette event in Illinois, to the amazement of Duntov and Shinoda, who were both sure the car had met its end a decade or so before.

Even more amazing is the fact that Duntov had next to nothing to do with the XP-819 project. Credit for the idea belonged to Frank Winchell, then chief of the Corvair engineering program. At the time Ralph Nader's Corvair-damning book, *Unsafe At Any Speed,* was still a year away and Winchell's enthusiasm concerning the performance potential of Chevrolet's little rear-engined compact was running high. Among his pet projects was a V-8 powered Corvair, a pro-

posal he hoped might also help vault him and his design team into the Corvette game. In Winchell's opinion, if a rear-mounted V-8 could work for a sporty Corvair application, why couldn't the same tactic succeed under Corvette guise?

Duntov didn't like the Corvair guy's idea, nor did stylist Bob McLean, especially since Winchell's initial drawings—based on a standard Sting Ray body—were downright ugly. Undeterred after a disappointing morning meeting with Duntov and McLean, Winchell then turned to his "styling expert," Larry Shinoda, who claimed he could make the design appealing. With the help of Allen Young and John Schinella, Shinoda did just that, returning right after lunch with a drawing that changed Duntov's and McLean's minds. "Where did you cheat?" Duntov reportedly asked.

With the go-ahead given, Winchell, Shinoda, and crew wasted little time; two months and a reported $500,000 later,

XP-819 was a rolling reality demonstrating both an innovative rear-engined chassis and prophetic styling. Although various small details were right off the Corvette parts shelf, Shinoda's fiberglass shell was something totally new, its soon-to-be familiar "Coke-bottle" figure, Kamm-back tail, and wedge-shaped, pointed nose predicting styling queues later used on the restyled 1968 Corvette. Signs of things to come also included the XP-819's lift-off top, side-guard door beams, and body-colored urethane front bumper, which would appear as a standard Corvette feature in 1973. Interior innovations included footpedals that adjusted electrically to meet the driver's reach, and molded door panels that became part of the seats when closed.

Beneath Shinoda's attractive fiberglass skin was a steel "backbone" frame built by a team of fabricators under the direction of engineer Larry Nies. Disc brakes and coil springs were used at all four corners, but the real news was the 287ci alloy V-8 suspended rearward in back from a modified Pontiac Tempest two-speed automatic transaxle. Although relatively lightweight compared to the typical cast-iron V-8s of its day, the XP-819's experimental small-block still represented more than enough mass to tip the scales in favor of a distinct tail-end weight bias—reportedly, 70 percent of the car's 2,700lb rested on the rear wheels.

Duntov had been skeptical from the beginning, figuring the tail-heavy XP-819 would be a bear to handle in the turns. Shinoda begged to differ, claiming the car's specially mismatched tires would compensate, within reason, for the extreme weight imbalance. Two-piece alloy wheels, the same used on Jim Hall's Chaparral racers, mounted special-order Firestone rubber that was the same diameter front and rear, but considerably wider in back. As Shinoda later told *Road & Track*'s Ray Thursby, "like a mid-engined Can-Am car, when you overcook it, it's damn hard to catch. But driving it normally, the XP-819 worked pretty well."

Normal driving, however, never has been a Corvette selling point, and it's doubtful the average driver would have been able to adjust to the XP-819 prototype's unique control characteristics. According to former Chevrolet engineer Paul Van Valkenburg, "the car could be set up to handle properly on a skid pad

in steady-state cornering, but transient or dynamic response was nearly uncontrollable at the limit." Proof of Van Valkenburg's claim was apparently supplied when a driver plowed the XP-819 into a test-track guard rail in 1965, although Shinoda was quick to point out that the accident occurred because the car was rolling on standard narrow street tires at the time. Regardless, Chevrolet gave up on Winchell's rear-engined Corvette idea almost overnight following the crash—as if it really had been seriously considered at all. From there, the plot truly thickened.

With even less fanfare than it received during its short, somewhat mysterious testing career, what was left of Winchell's XP-819 was quietly rolled out Chevrolet Engineering's back door, like many other GM performance experiments, to legendary race car builder Smokey Yunick's shop in Daytona Beach, Florida. Chevrolet general manager Bunkie Knudsen agreed to Yunick's request for the prototype with the understanding Smokey would salvage certain XP-819 parts for a Chevy-powered Indy car project he was working on, then trash the rest. By no means did Chevro-

Long-time race car builder Smokey Yunick, shown here on Florida's Daytona Beach in 1956. Notice the pre-1955 style wheel covers on this 1956 Corvette speedster. Yunick's Daytona Beach shop, the so-called "best damned garage in town," was home to many of Chevrolet's high-performance development projects, including the legendary "Mystery Motor" Mk II big-block V-8s that turned all heads during the 1963 Daytona 500. Yunick's garage also became the apparent final resting place for the XP-819 prototype when Chevrolet officials allowed Smokey to take possession only after he agreed to cut the rear-engined experiment into pieces. A collector later found those pieces in 1976, salvaged the mess and restored the unique piece of Corvette history. Daytona International Speedway photo

Total weight for XP-819 was roughly 2,700lb, with 70 percent of those pounds perched on the car's fat rear tires. Hard acceleration was not advised since that extreme rearward weight bias could quickly translate into a serious wheelstand that would make a veteran rail dragster pilot proud.

let brass intend for the rear-engined Corvette to survive, at least not in one piece.

Yunick, however, had other plans, and hitting the Brickyard with XP-819 remnants was not one of them. Some twenty-five years later, he confessed to *Corvette Fever* contributor Terry Jackson, explaining that his request for parts was only a ruse of sorts. "It didn't make sense to me that the car should be destroyed when Duntov was saving those CERV cars," he said. "I was building an Indy car and I concocted a story that I needed parts off the [XP-819] Corvette. They went for that."

Almost. Yunick's hope for preserving a piece of Corvette history were quickly squelched by a GM legal department order directing him to cut XP-819 into four pieces and document the dissection with a notarized photo. Captured on film as directed, the operation finally occurred in January 1973. From there, the pieces were stashed away to collect dust in a paint booth, where they were discovered by Missouri Corvette enthusiast Steve Tate in 1976 during one of Yunick's renowned "garage sales."

Tate bought the mess, which included nearly all the original components save for the 287ci alloy small-block V-8. Working almost blind, since GM people weren't interested in supplying any support—remember, as far as they knew, XP-819 had been "shredded" as ordered—he restored XP-819 as best he could, substituting a 350hp 327 for the missing original engine. All other details were put back as correctly as could be surmised under the circumstances, right down to the nonfunctional hideaway headlights which were nonessential (from a prototype perspective); motor drives were never installed in 1964. Overall, the restoration wasn't exactly perfect, but then again, neither was the original. Tate's project was completed in time for the 1978 Bloomington Gold show, where the majority of Corvette followers simply walked right by without so much as a nod in recognition, an understandable situation considering the event represented the odd prototype's first public appearance.

Tate sold his rear-engined Corvette to Terry Dahmer in the late 1980s, who a few years later passed it on to well-known Duesenberg collector Rick Carroll in southern Florida. Following Carroll's death in a 1989 auto accident, the prototype was bought at auction in May 1990 by Hallandale, Florida, exotic car dealer Marvin Friedman, who went out of business in 1991. Legal entanglements have since driven the unique rear-engined Corvette underground once more—a somewhat fitting fate for the mystery machine known as XP-819.

Michigan. Although paint and fiberglass panel quality would remain inconsistent through the years, many noticed a higher-grade look in 1964.

"There was some criticism of the quality of the fiberglass body when the Sting Ray first appeared," read *Road & Track*'s report, "but we were unable to find any ripples or other faults on our test car. Furthermore, the other characteristics normally associated with fiberglass, such as a tendency toward drumming and magnification of noise, were not present at all." Concerning that tendency, *Motor Trend*'s Bob McVay was suitably impressed by the improved Sting Ray shell. "Although previous Corvettes had some noise problems with their fiberglass bodies," he wrote, "we're happy to report that ours was as quiet as a sedan—no squeaks, no rattles, no resonance."

Like its body, the 1964 Corvette's interior showed few changes. As *Car Life* described it, "a pair of giant 6-in. dials, styled to look for all the world like the snuggly side of Jayne Mansfield's Maidenform, dominates the instrument cluster and registers (quite accurately, too) speed and rpm. Other instruments, scattered about like a meterorite-pocked moonscape, continue this inverted cone motif." Once more responding to customer complaints, designers did trade the instrument's reflective silver center sections for glare-resistant flat-black pieces. Minor modifications were also made to the bucket seat upholstery, and a simulated woodgrain-rim steering wheel became standard.

Beneath the hood, Corvette buyers had a choice of four 327 small-blocks, only this time the output ante was upped for the top two engines. The yeoman 250hp 327 remained the standard powerplant, as did a three-speed manual transmission. The optional L75 300hp 327 and Powerglide automatic carried over from 1963 as well. From there, however, the 1964 power lineup was upgraded significantly.

At the top was the L84 327 topped by its Rochester fuel-injection setup. Producing fifteen more horses than its 360hp predecessor, the 1964 L84 featured revised heads with bigger valves (2.02 inch intakes, 1.60 inch exhausts) and a new mechanical camshaft with longer duration and more lift, 0.485 inch, compared to the previous Duntov cam's 0.394/

Originally, the XP-819 was powered by an aluminum 287ci V-8, but that engine disappeared after the car went from Chevrolet Engineering into the hands of famed Daytona Beach race car builder Smokey Yunick. When XP-819 was restored in the late 1970s, a conventional iron-block 350hp 327 V-8 was used in place of the missing alloy small-block.

Above, left
Chevrolet's Sting Ray had been in the works well before Jaguar's E-type debuted in 1961, but many among the press couldn't help circulating rumors claiming Bill Mitchell's men had copied the British sports car's lines. The rumors were false, but that didn't stop the inevitable comparisons, some not so flattering. According to Car Life's August 1964 issue, "the Sting Ray's appearance is certainly striking, though it has been said to resemble a Jaguar XK-E with hiccups."
Below, left
Corvette customers began to favor the convertible Sting Ray in 1964, with sales of coupes topping out at 8,304 models, compared to the 13,925 convertibles built. Base price for a 1964 coupe was $4,252. Saddle Tan, RPO number 932, was one of seven exterior colors offered in 1964. The others were Tuxedo Black (900), Silver Blue (912), Daytona Blue (916), Riverside Red (923), Ermine White (936), and Satin Silver (940). This paint lineup was a carryover from 1963 save for the last color, which replaced the extra-cost Sebring Silver, RPO 941. Notice the optional backup lights, RPO T86, which carried a $10.80 price tag in 1964.

0.399 inch intake/exhaust specs. Since the added lift meant the valves were intruding farther into the combustion chamber, machined reliefs were required for the piston tops, which in turn meant a slight reduction in compression to 11:1. As in 1963, L84 exhaust manifolds were larger and more efficient than those used on the 250 and 300hp 327s.

L84 performance for 1964 easily convinced the small dogs to stay on the porch. A heavily optioned Sting Ray fuelie with 4.11:1 gears tested by *Motor Trend* went 0–60mph in 5.6 ticks of the clock, then stormed through the quarter-mile in 14.2sec at 100mph. After producing similar results at the strip, *Car Life*'s editors came away with nothing but praise for the fuel-injected 327: "Once underway, the engine exhibits a smoothness that was akin to turbines, with a fantastically sensitive throttle response that is unmatched by anything else produced in this country. Moreover, throttle response

While the 1964 Corvette's two lower-powered 327s remained as carryovers from 1963, the L84 fuelie received 15 more horsepower and the 340hp L76 was replaced by a much more aggressive 365hp version. Shown here is the 300hp L75 327, which again was priced at $53.80 and also repeated as the most popular power choice—10,471 were sold. Note the incorrect, owner-installed finned valve covers; as in 1963, both the base 250hp 327 and the 300hp L75 wore painted valve covers in 1964, while the 365hp L76 and 375hp L84 received the flashier finned pieces.

is instantaneous; there are no ragged spots while the rev counter swings hurriedly around the dial as the accelerator pedal is mashed to the floorboard."

Basically the same engine as the 375hp L84, with a big Holley four-barrel in place of fuel injection, the 1964 Corvette's second strongest 327, RPO L76, was advertised at 365hp, the highest output Chevrolet would record for its car-

The simulated woodgrain steering wheel, a Corvette option in 1963, became standard in 1964. Among other things, minor interior modifications also included exchanging the black plastic door knob used in 1963 with a chrome-plated piece for 1964. Ample storage space behind those buckets remained an attractive Sting Ray feature, although not all were enthused about the route required for baggage to enter that compartment. "Access to this space is through the doors alone," reported Road & Track, "which is extremely awkward when bulky items are concerned, and if the rear window could be hinged in Aston Martin style it would be a great improvement." Options appearing here include the M20 four-speed, priced at $188.30, and the $176.50 AM/FM radio, RPO U69.

bureted 327 small-block. In 1964, 7,171 buyers chose the $107.60 L76 option, while the L84's healthy $538 asking price helped keep total fuel-injection numbers down to 1,325. Production of 300hp L75 327s, priced at $53.80, was 10,471, and 3,262 customers stayed with the standard 250hp V-8.

As in 1963, the wimpy Powerglide automatic transmission couldn't be mated to the L76 or L84 327s. Although the standard three-speed manual was apparently listed early on as being available behind the two solid-lifter small-blocks, records show no such combinations, and the three-speed reportedly became "N.A." (not available) for the 365 and 375hp engines after January 1, 1964. L76 and L84 327s did get the M20 Muncie close-ratio four-speed, while the L75 and the 250hp standard 327 could have been bolted up to the optional wide-ratio M20.

Once more, 3.36:1 gears were standard for the two calmer, hydraulic-lifter small-blocks, with a shorter 3.70:1 ratio specified along with the L76 and L84 options. Bonneville-bound L76 or L84 buyers could have picked the optional 3.08:1 highway flyers (in a Positraction differential), while gears of choice for solid-lifter street warriors were the ever-popular 4.11:1 cogs. Serious Saturday night soldiers could have chosen the gut-wrenching 4.56:1 ratio.

The M20 four-speed was built in Muncie, Indiana, and featured an aluminum case, wider-faced gears, and larger synchronizers, and was both beefier and smoother than the old Borg-Warner four-speed it had replaced midyear in 1963. *Car Life* called it "a faultless gearbox." Bob McVay was convinced Chevrolet's new four-speed was "one of the best we've tested." Continued McVay in his September 1964 *Motor Trend* review, "it gives lightning-fast shifts, up or down, without ever hanging up, [and] it has short, positive throws between gears."

Additional performance options included the $43.05 G81 Positraction differential—ordered again, as in 1963, by 82 percent of Corvette buyers—and the rare $202.30 N03 36.5gal gas tank, installed in thirty-eight 1964 Sting Ray coupes. Two extra-cost features promised in 1963, off-road exhausts and the five cast-aluminum 15x6in knock-off wheels found under RPO P48, actually did appear in 1964, the Kelsey-Hayes knock-offs adding a tidy $322.80 to the Corvette sticker. That high price, combined with continued tire sealing problems, helps explain why only 806 P48 sets were sold.

Priced at $37.70, off-road exhausts, RPO N11, consisted of a low-restriction muffler with its own tailpipe in place of the standard muffler-tailpipe combo. Other than welded front joints (stock mufflers used clamps), the N11 system was externally identical to the standard pieces. The difference came inside the N11 muffler, where only three baffles were present, compared to the five found in the regular-issue mufflers. Fewer baffles meant lower back pressure, as well as a much more prominent exhaust note, both results representing music to performance buyers' ears.

Although N11 could be ordered along with the 375hp L84, 365hp L76, and 300hp L75/M20 powertrains, it wasn't available for the standard 250hp 327, nor the L75/M35 combination since these engines used 2in exhaust pipes. Off-road mufflers fit larger 2.5 inch pipes, which the manual-transmission 300hp 327s and the two solid-lifter small-blocks used. Another hot exhaust option, this one featuring sexy side-mount pipes, was planned for 1964 production, but didn't arrive until 1965.

New options on the 1964 list included the $75.35 K66 ignition and $86.10 F40 suspension. Installed only on the high-performance L76 and L84 327s, RPO K66 replaced the ignition's conventional points and condenser with a solid-state, transistorized system. Only 552 buyers checked off the K66 option during its first year. Much more rare, the F40 heavy-duty suspension became available in late January 1964 and was officially offered only with the 375hp 327, although F40 equipped L76 Corvettes are known. Among F40 heavy-duty components were beefier springs, stiffer shocks, and a thicker front stabilizer measuring 0.94in, as opposed to the standard 0.75in sway bar. F40 production was a mere eighty-two units.

Returning for an encore in 1964 were the J65 metallic brakes, a welcomed option that this time also included the J50 power brake booster. In 1963, an average customer could have ordered J50 and J65

This shot of a prototype 1964 Corvette wheel cover demonstrates the difference between the chrome-plated and frosted wheel covers.

separately for a Sting Ray at a total cost of $80.75. The following year Joe Average could have had the same power-assisted metallic brakes by simply checking off RPO J65 alone—and spent only $53.80 while doing it. It was a great deal, one that 4,780 '64 Corvette buyers couldn't pass up. And anyone who doubted J65's value needed only pick up a car magazine, *any* car magazine, for further convincing.

"Though production drum brakes (with organic linings) have been as prone to fade as any other on Detroit cars," read an August 1964 *Car Life* report, "opting for the metallic linings will let Sting Ray buyers avoid this problem." In *Road & Track*'s opinion, "to match performance, the [stock] brakes are adequate for normal fast driving but they will definitely fade and become uneven when used to the limit. When one considers both the weight and speed of the Sting Ray, it would appear to be an excellent car for a disc brake system, and it is surprising that

General Motors has not yet adopted discs for this model."

While discs were still a year away, there was one more high-performance Corvette brake option in 1964, but it didn't come cheap. Carrying a formidable $629.50 asking price, RPO J56 picked up where RPO Z06 left off in 1963. J56 equipment included the Z06's special sintered cerametalix brake linings, finned drums, internal drum-cooling fans, elephant-ear backing plate scoops, and unique dual-circuit master cylinder with power assist. Even though dealers had taken orders for Z06 Corvettes in the fall of 1963, the option wasn't carried over for 1964, but in fact was broken up into individual components. Having established that heavy-duty suspension was available as RPO F40 and that the special

brakes were then listed under RPO J56, a dealer bulletin dated December 26, 1963, detailed the new arrangement:

"In connection with the release of the above options [F40 and J56], your attention is directed to the special performance package (RPO Z06) initially released for the 1964 model Corvette. The contemplated design modifications and refinements did not materialize. However, in line with customers and dealer requests, the basic performance suspension and brake components have been separated and re-released as indicated above. Thus,

the customer can now select the option that meets his particular requirements or order both of them depending on the intended usage of his Corvette.

Above
Bigger valves and internal improvements to the Rochester fuel-injection unit helped boost the L84 327's output to 375hp in 1964. As the price for RPO L84 jumped to $538, demand fell considerably, with production dropping to 1,325. Notice the J50 power brake booster, a $43.05 option. RPO J50 production for 1964 was 2,270.

Right
In response to customer complaints about reflective glare, black instrument centers replaced the silver centers used in 1963. Also notice the 6500-rpm tach redline, a standard feature when either the 365hp L76 or 375hp L84 327s were ordered. The four-speed stick shown here is tied to a close-ratio M20 transmission. Production of the close-ratio M20 four-speed, used behind the L76 and L84 only, was 8,496 in 1964. Another 10,538 wide-ratio M20s were installed behind the base 327 and the 300hp L75.

Left
More than one wheel cover finish was used in 1964. Apparently early 1964 Corvettes were equipped with wheel covers featuring a chromed center section and a "frosted" grey-painted rim. This Silver Blue fuel-injected Corvette convertible wears the reversed "frosted" wheel covers used later. Notice the center is painted while the rim is chromed.

WE MAKE VERY FEW CORVETTES LIKE THIS

Look closely. Those are cast aluminum wheels. They're one of several optional-at-extra-cost performance items Corvette supplies to the handful of enthusiasts who demand them.

If you want a 36.5-gallon gas tank, we have it. There are special performance equipment packages too. They include heavy-duty brake and suspension parts, and they're available only with the 375-hp Ramjet fuel-injected V8, 4-speed shift and Positraction equipment.

Why all these extra-cost options for a handful of enthusiasts? Well, we built the Corvette Sting Ray when we found that not everybody wants the same kind of car. And the options came in when we found that not everybody wants the same kind of Corvette. Options let you get just the Corvette you want. To the exact degree.

You can't fit people to the car. So we fit the car to the people....Chevrolet
Division of General Motors. Detroit, Michigan. '64 CORVETTE STING RAY

Originally offered in 1963, these Kelsey-Hayes cast-aluminum knock-off wheels did not make regular production until 1964 thanks to various casting defects that resulted in poor tire sealing. Price for a set of five knock-offs, listed under RPO P48, was $322.80. Only 806 sets were sold in 1964. Notice the reference to the $202.30 N03 36.5gal fuel tank, itself a rare option. RPO N03 production was a mere 38.

"Some zones have orders in their Special Z06 Suspense File that they were instructed to hold by dealers. It is requested that zones immediately contact each dealer regarding such orders to determine exactly what type of performance equipment the customer wants. The zone should then delete Z06 as originally specified on the dealer's order and use the blank space(s) on the order form to indicate the performance option(s) the customer desires."

Officially, the J56 heavy-duty brake option was listed only for L84 Corvette customers in 1964, but like the F40 suspension equipment, it too has been found on L76 Sting Rays. Total production of J56 equipped 1964 Corvettes was a mere twenty-nine, including the fuel-injected coupe wearing knock-offs that floored Bob McVay of *Motor Trend*.

"Stopping power was amazing and adequate for the car's red-hot performance," he wrote. "We put it through stop after grueling stop from speeds of 100mph up to 134mph, and the brakes never faded completely. They smelled terrible and they'd pull slightly when hot, but they cooled down quickly and kept working no matter how much we asked of them."

"Oh, joy! What brakes!" screamed *Car Life*, calling all other binders "puny" in comparison. Nonetheless, *Car Life*'s report still questioned whether or not J56 advantages were worth $629. "Dissipation of the rapidly built-up heat in these brakes is, of course, hastened by the special drums," it explained, "but there is no reason to suspect that the stock drums with metallic linings wouldn't do substantially as well in less severe service." McVay questioned the cost, too, but for a different reason. "Somehow, we can't help feeling that four-wheel discs would be more practical, and we hear they're slated for 1965." He heard right.

Yet another new-and-improved fiberglass two-seater for 1965 would both stop and go better than any of its forerunners. But until it arrived on the scene, the 1964 Sting Ray was the best Corvette yet. As *Car Life* concluded in the summer of 1964, "there is no more go-able, road-able, steerable, adjustable, comfortable, respondable, or stoppable car mass-produced in this country today." Period.

Along with Dr. Dick Thompson and Bob Bondurant, Dick Guldstrand stood out as one of the most prominent Sting Ray race pilots in the early 1960s. Here, Guldstrand does his thing at Riverside, California, in April 1964. After a wheel fail-ure resulted in a serious end-over-end wreck at Riverside in 1963, a roller skate was attached to Guldstrand's roll bar as a joke. It would become his trademark. Dave Friedman photo

Chapter Five

1965

Easy Come, Easy Go

At first glance, it appeared nothing all that different awaited Corvette customers at new-model introduction time in the fall of 1964. Slight exterior variations on the Sting Ray theme included a revised, blacked-out grille; a reformed, totally flat hood devoid of those disliked indentations present in 1963 and 1964; re-arranged fender "gills" with three functional vertical louvers; restamped mag-type wheel covers; and restyled rocker trim with only one black line running end to end. Inside, plusher, reupholstered vinyl buckets offered a little more support, while a switch from conical instrument faces to a fully flat style helped drivers view the dashboard in a better light. Seatbelt retractors, molded door panels with integral armrests, a few reshaped baubles here and there, and that was basically it—Chevrolet's new Corvette for 1965. If prospective buyers never turned beyond page one, that's all they saw.

But the 1965 Sting Ray's storybook couldn't be judged solely by its dust jacket. Introduction of Chevrolet's third-edition Sting Ray marked the debut for a long-awaited standard feature, while the end of the model run spelled farewell for a long-revered performance option. Disc brakes—true state-of-the-art, world-class, bolted-to-the-ground binders—were finally added to the Corvette's arsenal in 1965, and not only up front, but at all four corners. Meanwhile, Rochester fuel injection, the famed fuelie equipment, was dropped from the Corvette's list of extra-cost power sources after 1965.

And if all that wasn't enough front-page news for Sting Ray followers, 1965 also brought the Corvette's first big-block V-8, the brutish 396 Turbo-Jet—425 horses worth of tire-melting muscle more than capable of helping lead-footed, hell-bent drivers forget all about the fuelie's eminent demise. An obvious response to escalating enemy activity in Detroit's heated battle for cubic-inch supremacy, the 396ci Mark IV V-8 debuted as a Sting Ray option in February and quickly left larger big-block rivals in the dust thanks in part to its innovative "porcupine" cylinder heads. Not since 1963 had there been so many high-powered headlines on the fiberglass front.

No slouches when it came to burning rubber, Duntov's fuel-injected small-block V-8s had been the Corvette's crown jewels since 1957. Manufactured by Rochester Products, a GM division in Rochester, New York, the Ramjet continuous-flow fuel-injection system was originally the work of engineer John Dolza, who first

Corvette colors numbered eight in 1965; Tuxedo Black, Ermine White, Nassau Blue, Glen Green, Milano Maroon, Rally Red, Goldwood Yellow, and Silver Pearl. This maroon coupe is one of 771 1965 Sting Rays equipped with the 375hp L84 fuel-injected 327, the last of the famed fuelie Corvettes.

Although they were developed by the Kelsey-Hayes company, the 1965 Corvette's standard four-wheel disc brakes were manufactured by Delco. Representing state-of-the-art stopping power, at least from an American perspective, these standard brakes could still be deleted by Corvette buyers who preferred to live in the past. RPO J61 both replaced those discs with drums and put $64.50 back into a customer's pocket as a credit. Notice the short section of emergency brake cable appearing just in front of the rear disc at right. The Corvette design cleverly incorporated the center of that rotor assembly as a drum for a conventional parking brake.

developed a working unit in 1955, hot on the heels of Mercedes' announcement of standard fuel injection for its classic gull-wing 300SL in 1954. Driven to make the

Corvette a world-class competitor, chief engineer Ed Cole then put Duntov on the project in 1956, reportedly telling him that if he wasn't so busy running things, he'd be right there in the shop working with Dolza on fuel-injection development. Not long afterward, Cole was promoted to general manager of Chevrolet and GM vice president; six months later, the regular-production Ramjet fuel-injected unit was introduced.

Early Ramjet fuel injection certainly had its share of bugs, but performance was exceptional with the temperamental unit in top tune. Two varieties were offered, 250 and the 283hp, atop the newly enlarged 283ci V-8 for 1957. Of the 283hp Corvette, *Road & Track* reported that "the fuel-injection engine is an ab-

solute jewel, quiet and remarkably docile when driven gently around town, yet instantly transformable into a roaring brute when pushed hard. Its best feature is its instantaneous throttle response, completely free of any stutter or stumble under any situation." Zero to 60 for the 283hp fuelie came in a mere 5.7sec—fast even by today's standards, downright frightening relative to what Detroit was building some thirty-five years ago.

Continued development helped iron out bugs and boost performance as fuel-injection reliability improved and maximum fuel-injection horsepower grew: 290hp in 1958, 315 in 1961, 360 in 1962, and 375 in 1964. At the same time, fuelie production varied, from 1,040 units in 1957, up to 1,511 in 1958, down to

359 in 1960, followed by a steady upward trend reaching a peak of 2,610 for the 1963 Sting Ray. That trend turned back down the following year, with fuelie sales dropping to 1,325, then 771 for 1965.

Helping bring about the demise of fuel injection was the development of bigger, better four-barrel carburetors and improved intake manifolds, which made Chevrolet's conventionally aspirated, yeoman-like V-8s nearly as powerful as their more expensive, finicky fuelie brethren. The appearance in 1964 of the truly formidable 365hp L76 327 perhaps represented the straw that broke fuel injection's back. Handwriting on the wall quickly followed.

"If you have fuel injection on your Corvette," scrawled Ed Janicki in *Car Life's* November 1964 issue, "you have some sort of distinction. Few late model Corvette owners have it, even though it's been available from Chevrolet for about eight years now." Janicki's explanation for the decline? "If you bought a fuel-injection system this year you know that it cost you as much as a vacation to the World's Fair," he claimed. "Fuel injection is becoming less appealing for just that reason—price. Sports car enthusiasts don't feel they're getting their money's worth. As an example, the highest rated Chevrolet engine (365bhp) costs only $107 extra. Put fuel injection on that engine and it goes to 375bhp. That's only 10bhp more and you have to pay $538 to get it . . . $53 for each additional horsepower."

Fuel injection had never come cheap, but at least the price had remained the same, at $484.20, from 1957 to 1962. RPO L84's cost was even cut to $430.40 in 1963. However, the L84 option's limited-production status forced Chevrolet to tack on that $107.60 price increase in 1964, and as a result the percentage of fuel-injection installations dropped by half, from 12 percent in 1963 to 6 percent the following year. By late 1964 it was clear the fuelie's days were numbered. As *Motor Trend's* clairvoyants predicted in their December 1964 issue, "Chevrolet will probably drop fuel injection on [its] 1966 Corvettes. Fewer and fewer buyers are ordering it. Chevy's officials feel [$538 is] too much to pay for an extra 10hp and slightly better throttle response. Looks like [fuel injection] could go

the way of air suspension and swivel seats." That it did.

Before it left, however, Corvette fuel injection did have one last dance in 1965, and its partners were, as usual, quite impressed, especially after the standard four-wheel discs joined the party. "Ten years ago, who could have guessed that the 1965 Corvette would have fuel injection, 4-speed manual transmission, limited slip differential, all independent suspension and, wonder of wonder, disc brakes?" read *Road & Track's* report on a 1965 375hp L84 coupe with F40 suspension and the 3.70:1 Positraction differential. "The Corvette has become a car any manufacturer would be proud to produce, and a far, far cry from the 6-cyl phut-phut with [a] 2-speed automatic transmission that was standard in the first model to bear the Corvette name."

Proving the Rochester unit hadn't lost a step, *Road & Track's* testers managed 0-60mph in 6.3sec, with the end of the quarter-mile coming up 8.1sec later. Trap speed was 99mph. As usual, a confident launch contributed greatly to the 1965 L84's 14.4sec elapsed time (ET). Reported *Road & Track*, "making a fast start, thanks to good weight distribution, independent rear suspension and Positraction, the big machine simply squats and squirts."

Leaving their mess behind, *Road & Track's* fuelie fans walked away all smiles.

"Summing up, the car does a masterful job of hitting the market bulls-eye. [It's] keyed to the boulevardier sports/racey types who account for the great majority of its sales. It has enough pizzazz for a movie set, or crumpet collecting, or nymphet nabbing, or for the types who get their jollies from looking at all that glitter. It encourages the Walter Mittys to become Fangios or Foyts. Yet it also goes well enough to suit the driver who is sincere about going fast, and can handle that much performance with skill."

Ten years later, *Road & Track's* nostalgic staff remained impressed enough to take another look at Chevrolet's last fuel-injected Corvette. Though obviously enhanced in relation to a perspective based on experiences with the ho-hum collection of so-called performance machines being built in 1975, *Road & Track's* retroactive response was still well worth reading:

Basically an L84 327 with a big Holley four-barrel carburetor in place of the Rochester fuel-injection unit, the 365hp L76 was introduced in 1964 and carried over unchanged into 1965. This airbrushed piece of factory artwork simply added the L76 features to an earlier image of a 1963 small-block. In 1965, 5,011 Corvette customers shelled out an extra $129.15 for RPO L76, which could only be ordered with the close-ratio Muncie four-speed.

Left
A blacked-out grille, revised rocker moldings and restyled fender louvers set the 1965 Corvette apart from its predecessors. As in 1964, coupes again represented a distinct minority in 1965, with production reaching 8,186. Base price for a 1965 coupe was $4,321. Options shown here include the $134.50 sidemount exhausts (RPO N14), $322.80 knock-off wheels (P48), and $50.05 "goldwall" nylon-cord tires (T01). RPO P48 sales for 1965 totaled 1,116, with 130 of these knock-off sets wearing the 7.75x15in gold-wall tires. Another 859 sets of the T01 tires were also sold on standard steel wheels.

"Once the revs begin to build up, hang on! By the time the big tach needle reaches 3000rpm, things are beginning to happen so fast it's dizzying. The fuel-injection cars always had the close-ratio 4-speed gearbox; this car had the numerically high 4.11:1 final drive ratio, which makes the most of the close ratios. Even with the 4.11 it takes a good bit of clutch slipping to get the car off the line and it's a nice long climb to the redline at 54mph. But after that the driver works hard just to keep up with the engine, so fast does the redline come up in 2nd and 3rd, and it takes very little time to redline the engine in 4th gear either for that matter. The pull begins to fall off above 5500rpm, but it is a brilliant show up to that point."

After its retro road test, *Road & Track* couldn't help but ask the question how Chevrolet engineers could let mid-1960s peer pressures promoting more cubic inches over balanced performance convince them to let the polite, yet potent fuelie Corvette die in favor of a less-flexible, musclebound, big-block bully? "It seems funny, doesn't it, in the context of 1975 to remember that a leading manufacturer had airflow-controlled, continuous-flow fuel injection and dropped it? The Rochester system was just that, and though it was quite different in detail and designed for lot of power rather than low emissions, it answers the same basic description as the system now used on Volvos and Porsches, for instance, to meet 1975 emission regulations. How times change." Seven years later, fuel-in-

As in 1964, those vents in the roof pillar behind the door were functional for 1965 serving as exhausts for the electric ventilation system. Notice the backup lights; in 1965 they became a part of the Comfort and Convenience Group, RPO Z01. Priced at $16.16, RPO Z01 also included a day/night rearview mirror.

jection performance returned to the Corvette lineup, this time as standard equipment in the form of the 1982 200hp 350ci small-block with Cross-Fire Injection.

Of course, most Corvette buyers in 1965 probably would have agreed the arrival of disc brakes was ample consolation for the eventual loss of fuel injection at year's end. Car owners and critics alike had long been begging for better brakes, even more so after Studebaker made front discs standard in 1963 on its equally timeless fiberglass sportster, the Avanti. Duntov's crew weren't blind, nor deaf, it was just that development of suitably superior disc brakes for the Corvette required some suitably intensive, time-consuming testing.

If you'd just spent fifty miles twisting down a mountainside in this '65 CORVETTE, you'd be taking the words right out of our mouth about its new 4-wheel disc brakes.

Praise comes easily to Corvette's big caliper-type disc brakes. They're fade-resistant, heat-resistant, water-resistant and fuss-resistant.

Adjustment and maintenance? What adjustment and maintenance? These discs can get along swell without much help.

All this peace of mind is standard equipment on all '65 Corvettes. But even this doesn't complete the improvements.

We've added a new 327-cubic-inch V8. This new one is the best behaved

350-hp V8 you ever met. Loaded with all kinds of good things a high-performance engine ought to have. But tamed to a civilized purr. You can order it or a 300-, 365- or Ramjet fuel-injected 375-hp V8 on any Corvette.

As for appearance, it's brushed up. Smooth new hood, magnesium-style wheel covers, new grille design and functional front fender louvers. And a revised interior that treats you even more elaborately than before.

We didn't change all those lovely

items you can specify, like 4-Speed fully synchronized transmission, cast aluminum wheels, Positraction—the lot.

All in all, Corvette for '65 adds up to a lot more car in every way. Which we think is the best possible reason for changing it.

Chevrolet Division of General Motors, Detroit, Michigan

Chevrolet ads in the fall of 1964 couldn't say enough about the Sting Ray's standard disc brakes, news that would soon be overshadowed by the debut of the Corvette's first big-block V-8 in the spring of 1965. Notice the reference to the equally new 350hp L79 small-block. In Car and

Driver's opinion, dropping the wonderfully docile, wildly energetic L79 beneath the fiberglass hood of a $4,500 car with four-wheel discs and independent rear suspension represented one of the best buys on the sports car market, Europe included.

Automotive disc brake designs date back almost as far as automotive history itself, with England's Frederick William Lanchester taking out the first patent for such a setup in 1902. Various approaches to the idea followed over the years, but disc brake development truly got rolling

once WWII military men began looking for suitable ways to haul down heavy, high-powered aircraft during landings. Both Lockheed , a renowned US aircraft manufacturer, and England's Girling firm had entered the game in the 1930s, while another British outfit, the Dunlop Rubber

Company, stopped everyone in their tracks after the war with its own ground-breaking disc brake design that established standards still used today.

In 1951, Girling bought a license to produce the Dunlop design for passenger-car applications. Equipped with Girling brakes, a team of C-type Jaguar roadsters brought worldwide acclaim for the innovative binders by winning the 24 Hours of Le Mans in 1953, embarrassing Enzo Ferrari's much faster V-12 coupes in the process. Two years later, all British racing machines featured disc brakes, as did Ferrari by 1958. Across the Atlantic, Chrysler and Crosley each offered a somewhat crude disc brake system in 1949.

General Motors' experiments with disc brakes began in 1937, although Detroit's advancements in the field lagged far behind what European engineers were doing to surely, safely stop their cars. After both Chrysler's and Crosley's designs failed to impress anyone, GM's Delco-Moraine Division did manage to produce an experimental disc brake system—featuring "ventilated" rotors for increased cooling capacity—in 1954, with working examples ending up on Pontiac's Firebird II gas turbine show car in 1956.

Halibrand discs were tested briefly on the Corvettes John Fitch took to Sebring in 1956, and Duntov chose Girling disc brakes for his lightweight racing Sting Rays late in 1962. Although Girling's competition-proven design couldn't handle the standard Corvette's weight, it was able to haul in the much lighter Grand Sport racers. Earlier that same year, Delco's four-wheel discs had been tested on a prototype Sting Ray at Sebring, and finally arrived as Corvette standard equipment in 1965.

Once development of Corvette discs got serious after 1962, it was primarily long-time test driver and engineer Bob Clift who helped make them a production reality. The Kelsey-Hayes company actually received the contract for developing the Corvette's four-wheel disc design, and it was the K-H people with whom Clift worked closely for three years. But when it came time to manufacture the resulting four-wheel disc brake equipment, Delco outbid Kelsey-Hayes.

Advantages of the Corvette's Delco discs were various, not the least of which was their fade resistance. Brake fade is a product of high heat, itself an inherent reality where friction is involved. Conventional drum brakes are especially sensitive to fade because they do not dissipate heat well, and thermal expansion tends to increase the clearance between drum wall and brake lining. Discs naturally develop less heat since they work "out in the open," with their caliper-activated friction pads and rotor faces fully exposed (dis-

Below
Introduced for 1965 as a milder version of the 365hp solid-lifter L76 327, this L79 small-block had civilized hydraulic lifters and 11:1 compression. Fed by a Holley four-barrel carburetor, the L79 327 produced 350hp at 5800rpm. Production of RPO L79 was 4,716, making the 350hp 327 the third most popular Corvette power choice in 1965 behind the 300hp L75 327, which found 8,356 buyers that year, and the 365hp L76. The L79's price was $107.60. Adding even more to this L79 coupe's original asking price was the optional air conditioning, RPO C60, which cost $421.80 in 1965. Air conditioning sales hit 2,423 that year, up nearly 25 percent from 1964.

Continuing a Corvette tradition, the 1965 Sting Ray's standard wheel cover featured a simulated knock-off spinner. Though certainly distinctive, the 1965 covers were not exactly loved by all.

According to Car Life's curbside critics, they were "less happy, for now they imitate not only knock-off hubs, but mag wheels as well."

You might have missed the fender badge, but you couldn't have overlooked the 1965 396 Sting Ray's bulging hood. Listed under RPO L78, the Corvette's first big-block V-8 produced 425 real horsepower. Checking off the L78 option meant adding $292.70 to a 1965 convertible's $4,106 base price. Total convertible production that year was 15,376, with 1,409 of those powered by the L78 396. Another 748 1965 coupes were built with the 425hp big-block V-8.

counting the presence of thin splash shields) to ambient air temperatures.

Heat build-up inside an internal-acting drum brake has no place to go unless such clever optional tricks as the Z06's finned drums, cerametalix linings, internal cooling fans, and vented-backing plates with air scoops were used. Adding the Z06 brakes in 1963, followed by their J56 counterparts in 1964, did greatly reduce operating temperatures, and thus fade, but the merits of all that extra baggage—

and its accompanying huge price tags—was rendered a moot point once four-wheel discs made the scene.

Described by *Motor Trend*'s Jim Wright as "fade-proof," the 1965 Corvette's discs were kept even cooler thanks to their aforementioned ventilated design. As opposed to some early disc brake arrangements that featured solid rotors, Delco rotors essentially were two separate discs joined together by webbing. Compared to racing discs which are

commonly drilled full of holes, Corvette discs were "hollow," meaning cooling air was able to flow through them with the same effect created by the racing-style holes. Standard American brakes in 1965 simply didn't come any cooler.

Another disc brake advantage involved the relationship between the driver's right foot and the road, a concept known as "pedal modulation." Conventional drum brakes are self-energizing, meaning that the energy used to stop a wheel from turning when the shoe comes in contact with the drum also helps squeeze that shoe against the drum. Although this effect translates into "free" stopping pressure, it also hinders pedal feel, as driver effort and actual braking power are not proportional. Among other things, a drum brake system's inherently weak pedal modulation relationship contributes to wheel lockup during hard stops. As Duntov told *Corvette News* in 1964, with the new disc brakes a

Corvette's "retardation is directly proportional to pedal pressure so that the driver can modulate his retardation very precisely. So the degree of braking control is much greater with discs than with self-energizing drum brakes."

Underlying all this was the plain fact that the Corvette disc brakes simply offered more pure stopping power, measured in part by total swept area, which is the amount of rotor face (multiplied by four) covered by the friction pads through one revolution. Like the drums they replaced, the Sting Ray's durable, cast-iron discs were big, measuring 11.75in in diameter and 1.25in in thickness. Effective lining area for each brake pad was about 20sq-in, translating into a total swept area of 461.2sq-in, up considerably from the 1964 drum brake system's 328sq-in. Mashing those pads against the rotors were four-piston calipers with 1.857in pistons in front, 1.375in out back. Stopping power was split 65/35, front to rear.

New bucket seat upholstery, inner door panels with integral armrests, and flat-faced gauges were among interior revamps for 1965. This 1965 fuelie coupe also features the $48.45 teakwood steering wheel and M20 close-ratio four-speed transmission, the only tranny offered behind the L84 327 in 1965. One popular option this coupe doesn't have is the $203.40 AM/FM radio, RPO U69. Ninety-four percent of Corvette buyers checked off RPO U69 in 1965.

As much as everyone in 1965 rushed to praise the Corvette's four-wheel discs, one thing did need to be said: the big Corvette drum brakes left behind weren't entirely bad. As *Car Life* explained in its August 1965 issue, "though the old standard drums were liberal in size and adequate for everyday stopping they weren't always even in their action and could be made to fade fairly easily; still, relative to the contemporary domestic production, they were among the better standard brakes available."

Even better were the optional J56 heavy-duty drum brakes. In their heyday, these beefy brakes easily represented state-of-the-art pieces, at least as far as American performance cars—as well as average American drivers—were concerned. As Duntov later told Karl Ludvigsen, author of *Corvette: America's Star-Spangled Sports Car,* "although brutal, [the J56 drums] had the highest energy-dissipating ability and durability of all brakes we could visualize on our Corvette." All that was forgotten, however, in 1965 as the Sting Ray's discs simply embarrassed everything else on U.S. roads.

In Bob McVay's opinion, "the 1965 Corvette has the finest, smoothest-acting, and strongest set of stoppers available on any American automobile." "Disc brakes are big news on the automotive scene this year," he wrote in *Motor Trend*'s April 1965 issue, "but Corvette builders don't believe in doing things halfway."

Stated a *Road & Track* report, "long ago we gave up (read chickened out) on doing stomp-down, all-out panic stops in American cars, but the Corvette restored our faith to such an extent that we did 0-80-0-80-0 time after time and grew bored, almost, with the ease and lack of fuss with which the car stopped straight and true. No lock up, no fade, no muscle-straining increases in pedal pressure. Just good dependable stops. Wonderful."

Even though those wonderful disc brakes were indeed included as standard equipment in 1965, the Sting Ray options list still carried the old drums as a $64.50 credit under RPO J61, basically so that Chevrolet could dispose of leftover supplies. Only 316 customers helped cut down the pile, however, leaving Chevy's idea guys poised to try again with their J61 "inventory clearance" in 1966; but the credit option did not return.

Options that did return for 1965 included the aluminum knock-off wheels; power brakes, steering, and windows; leather seats; air conditioning; F40 heavy-duty suspension; K66 transistorized ignition; N03 36.5gal fuel tank; and N11 off-road exhausts. Again offered as a coupe option only, RPO N03 was picked by a mere forty-one Corvette customers in 1965. Newly offered extra-cost items that year included a cockpit-controlled telescopic steering wheel (N36), an honest-to-goodness teakwood steering wheel

(N32), and another off-road exhaust system, the $134.50 N14 pipes. Priced at $48.45, the classy teakwood wheel was yet another Corvette option hinted at one year, then introduced the next.

Mentioned as well in 1964 paperwork, RPO N14 featured a pair of sexy, side-mount exhausts with crimped restrictor pipes (mufflers in name only) hidden behind bright aluminum heat shields. Installing the N14 system meant completely deleting the standard dual exhausts and replacing the rear body panel, its two lower openings no longer needed. Fiberglass modification was also required along the body's lower edge to make room for the installation, which when completed was not easily missed, either by eyes or ears. As much an appearance option as a performance feature, the N14 system was labeled "off-road" by Chevrolet in order to shirk liability for any noise ordinance violations. Whether included with a tried-and-true 327 small-block or the newly offered L78 396 Turbo-Jet, those side-mount exhausts didn't keep a secret very well at all. Neither could Chevrolet, in 1964, concerning the impending arrival of its new big-block V-8.

That summer the rumor mill was overloaded with speculation surrounding the return of Chevrolet's appropriately named Mystery Motor, an all-out racing big-block V-8 created by engineer Dick Keinath in July 1962. Keinath's Mystery Motor, officially known as the Mark II, was similar on the bottom end to Chevrolet's other clandestine racing big-block, the super-stock Z11 powerplant, also developed midyear 1962. Both powerplants featured identical displacements, 427ci, but that's where comparisons ended. While the Z11 drag-racing V-8 was old news—it was simply a highly modified, stroked 409—the Mark II big-block was like nothing else seen before, especially up top where a pair of exceptional, free-breathing cylinder heads featured innovative staggered valves laid out in a seemingly haphazard fashion reminiscent of a porcupine's quills. Dyno-measured output for the Mark II easily topped 500hp.

Literally laughing in the face of the AMA factory-racing ban, Chevrolet Engineering, in cahoots with veteran Daytona Beach speed merchant Smokey Yunick, prepared a Mark II stock car (one of five built) for the February 1963 running of

NASCAR's Daytona 500. General Motors top brass, however, got the last laugh when they sent down their infamous cease and desist memo in January. Having seen enough of Duntov's semi-secret Grand Sport shenanigans, as well as what was going on in Yunick's shop, GM chairman Frederick Donner brought both projects to a halt, but not before the Mark II made its record-shattering debut in Florida. As impressive as they had been during the two 100-mile Daytona 500 qualifiers on February 22 (a Mark II Chevy stocker won both, averaging in excess of 160mph), mechanical mishaps left the five Mystery Motor Chevrolets back in the pack while five Fords took top honors at Daytona's big show February 24. With all of GM's divisions then officially out of racing, Chevrolet's Mark II 427 was apparently headed for the scrap heap following its Daytona 500 failure.

Such was not the case. Regardless of GM's newfound anti-racing stance, the Mark II V-8's potential as a street performer wasn't overlooked. Equally hard to miss were the two 427-powered Corvette competition specials built late in 1962 at Mickey Thompson's shop in Long Beach, California. Driven by Bill Krause, one of these beasties took third in the Daytona Challenge Cup in January 1963, setting the stage for a possible production follow-up. But Duntov was not exactly thrilled about the prospect of a big-block Corvette, preferring instead to concentrate on much lighter powerplants with high horsepower-per-cubic-inch ratios; smaller, stronger engines better suited for his ideal of a tail-heavy Sting Ray. Nonetheless, he was overruled, and about a year after the Mystery Motor's Daytona debut, Zora found himself forming a special design team of engineers including Fred Frincke, Cal Wade, and Denny Davis. The team's goal? To build a street-going counterpart of the Mark II big-block, a major chunk of cast-iron guaranteed to tip the scales toward a Corvette's nose.

As it was, a Ford man may well have had more to do with the initial development of a big-block Corvette than Duntov. Carroll Shelby, former Le Mans winner and builder of the fastest "production" machine ever to hit the American road, quite simply forced Chevrolet's hand. In 1963, Shelby's Ford-powered AC Cobras eclipsed Duntov's Sting Rays on the American sports car racing front, although it wasn't exactly a fair fight. Shelby's Cobra was nearly a half ton lighter and wasn't even close to being a true production automobile, with only 1,003 built mostly by hand during the entire five-year model run—at its peak, the Corvette plant in St. Louis rolled that many Sting Rays off the line in two weeks. Regardless of this "apple-orange" situation, comparisons between America's only two-seat sportsters were continually made, and the Corvette continually got the short end.

Initially armed with a 260ci Ford Windsor small-block, followed by a 289ci Windsor, the lithe, beastly Cobra always held a distinct power-to-weight ratio advantage over the larger, heavier, much more civilized Corvette. That advantage grew by leaps and bounds late in 1964 when Shelby-American started stuffing Ford's NASCAR-proven 427ci Le Mans big-block V-8 beneath that little aluminum bonnet, instantly injecting 425 horses' worth of venom into the Cobra's bite. In or out of racing, Chevrolet had little choice but to retaliate.

Duntov's engineers were, of course, already working on a big-block Corvette when Shelby's outrageous 427 Cobra hit the streets. Grist for that ever-present rumor mill had been piling up all through 1964, then spilled out that fall. As *Motor Trend* claimed in its September issue, "Chevrolet may revive the Mark II Daytona engine for passenger car use. This is the engine that shook the troops at Daytona in 1963, developing about 550hp from 427 inches, giving lap speeds up to 166mph. It disappeared when GM dropped out of racing. But recent reports mention prototypes under test powered by this basic engine reduced to 396ci." *Motor Trend* readers were instructed to keep an eye out for this new big-block come spring.

As a Corvette ad announced just months into 1965, "You heard the rumors. Now hear this . . . There *is* a Turbo-Jet 396 from Chevrolet." *Sports Car Graphic*'s Jerry Titus almost couldn't believe it, writing that "while General Motors continues to pursue its non-racing policy and promote the theme of Proving Grounds Development as the ONLY answer, it is about to put an engine in production that was developed specifically for racing." Production of 396 Turbo-Jet

Like the L84 fuelie small-block, the 425hp L78 big-block could only be ordered with the close-ratio M20 Muncie four-speed. Mandatory options also included the K66 transistorized ignition and the G81 Positraction differential. This L78 convertible also has the optional J50 power brakes—notice the vacuum booster and dual-circuit master cylinder.

big-blocks began in January 1965, with the first Mark IV-equipped Chevrolets hitting the streets in April.

Chevrolet general manager Bunkie Knudsen made it all official in February during a press gathering at GM's Mesa, Arizona, proving grounds. Introduced to reporters was the Mark IV V-8, the downsized 396ci Mark II derivative mentioned by *Motor Trend*. Knudsen proudly pointed to three new big-blocks: a hydraulically timed 325hp Turbo-Jet for the topline Caprice; a 375hp 396 (also with hydraulic lifters) for the equally new Z16 Malibu, Chevrolet's first SS 396 Chevelle; and a solid-lifter, 425hp maximum Mark IV for the Corvette, which Titus then described as a "fiberglass porcupine," a reference to those wonderful, wild Mark IV cylinder heads.

The Mark IV head's staggered-valve porcupine arrangement was made possible by Chevrolet's trademark individually mounted ball-stud rocker arm design, a trick that had helped make Chevy's first overhead-valve V-8—the high-winding "Hot One"—so hot in 1955. Not only did those ball-stud rockers greatly reduce valvetrain weight, they also allowed engineers to put the valves where they would work

best. Instead of designing the all-important combustion chamber around a limited valve position, the ball-stud rockers' flexibility gave Duntov's crew a clean slate.

Mark IV intake valves were located up high near their ports and inclined slightly, making for a straighter flow from intake manifold to combustion chamber. An opposite inclination was applied (to a slightly lesser degree) on the exhaust end to the same effect. In between, those inclined valves opened into a "modified wedge" (some classified it as semi-hemispherical, semi-hemi for short) combustion chamber that featured improved flame propagation and superb volumetric efficiency. Along with exceptional breathing characteristics, the inclined valve setup also offered slightly more room for the Mark IV's truly big valves, 2.19in intake and 1.72in exhaust.

Activating those valves was a serious solid-lifter cam, a lumpy loper with a 0.497in lift on the intake side, 0.503in on exhaust. Duration was 348 degrees with a 127 degree overlap. Feeding coal to the Mark IV's fire was a job handled by a big Holley four-barrel carb atop an aluminum intake, while the K66 transistorized ignition—mandatory with the L78 option—

Since this fuel-injected 1965 coupe was ordered without an optional radio, there was no need for the ever-present ignition shielding required on a Corvette. As in 1964, the 1965 L84 327 produced 375hp at 6200rpm. Notice the dual-circuit master cylinder (bottom right) included as part of the J50 power brake package. This L84 small-block also has the optional K66 electronic ignition. Carrying a $75.35 price tag, RPO K66 found 3,686 buyers in 1965. Only 304 K66/L84 combos were sold, with seventeen of those cars built without the U69 radio.

Left
Engineer and Corvette test driver Bob Clift poses with a Canadian-built 1974 Bricklin SV-1—a gullwing creation he helped design—at a November 1993 Bricklin club meet in Orlando, Florida. The man behind the development of the Corvette's four-wheel disc brake system, Clift joined innovative independent automaker Malcolm Bricklin in Fredricton, New Brunswick, in 1973 after retiring from Chevrolet Engineering.

supplied the spark to start that fire. Inside the bores, impact-extruded aluminum pistons squeezed the fuel-air mixture to an octane-intensive 11:1 ratio. Free-flowing, header-type cast-iron exhaust manifolds directed spent gases down the pipes in short order.

Everything else about the 396 Turbo-Jet was beefier or better than your average big-block. The Mark IV's forged-steel crank (with cross-drilled journals for added lubrication) and rods were about as tough as they came, as was the block itself. Pumped up where it counted, on the bottom end, the L78 cylinder block featured huge bulkheads, massive bearing surfaces, and four-bolt main bearing caps. All this extra rigidity, combined with an exceptional lubrication system, relatively lightweight valvetrain, and excellent breathing characteristics translated into sky-high rev limits for the L78. Maximum

output of 425hp came on at 6400rpm, higher even than the 375hp L84 fuelie, which developed its top power at 200rpm less. Torque output for the L78 was 415lb-ft at 4000rpm.

Even with a slight displacement disadvantage, the 396 Turbo-Jet was an able opponent for anything Detroit could offer in 1965. As *Motor Trend*'s Roger Huntington wrote, the L78 "can't quite match the cubes of the '427' Ford or the '426-S' Dodge/Plymouth option, but breathing may be enough to more than make up the difference." *Motorcade*'s Jim Wright agreed, claiming Chevrolet's new big-block wasn't "as spectacular as the all-out racing engines from Ford and Chrysler, but as a high performance street engine it's going to be hard to beat."

Dropping the optional L78 big-block between fiberglass fenders for 1965 required various revamps, not the least of

which was an impressive bulging hood with functional louvers. Cooling the beast beneath that bulge meant adding a larger fan and a wider radiator with an appropriately large shroud. And like the K66 ignition, Chevrolet's close-ratio M20 four-

Corvette buyers who opted for the optional removable hardtop in 1965 numbered 7,787. Of that RPO C07 total, 1,277 were added at no cost in place of a folding top. Although the $236.75 hardtop was certainly attractive, it wasn't easy to handle. "Definitely not a one-man job," wrote Motor Trend's Bob McVay. "Taking off [the] top can be a chore. Once in place, it rattled and required lots of muscle to lift up in order to get into [the] luggage compartment." Ten years later, Road & Track remained displeased in a retro-review of a 1965 fuelie, claiming the removable hardtop required "a lot of bolting and unbolting to install or remove, and one assumes the body designers saw it as an all-winter proposition."

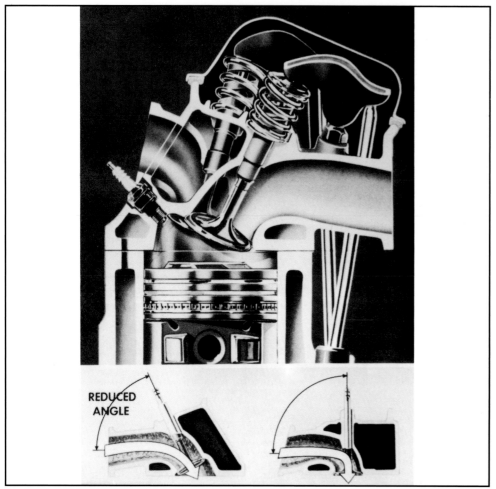

The 396ci Mk IV big-block V-8 featured innovative "porcupine" cylinder heads, a design that drew its name from the way the staggered, canted valves protruded up from the combustion chambers in varying angles akin to a porcupine's quills. Individual stamped-steel rocker arms allowed engineers to angle the valves towards their respective ports to minimize flow restriction caused by sharp bends in the intake and exhaust passages.

250hp 327 and optional 300hp L75 small-block carrying over from 1964. Although initial reports had the solid-lifter 365hp L76—also a 1964 carryover—being replaced midyear by the L78 396, such was not the case. A 1965 *Interim Shop Manual* did mention that planned small-block/big-block trade, but an announcement in the March edition of the *Chevrolet Service News* cleared up the confusion. "The important midyear change in engine lineup for Corvette is the addition of the extra-cost 425hp Turbo-Jet 396 V-8," it read. "Limited availability of the 365hp 327 V-8 is expected for the balance of the model year." L76 Turbo-Fire production did drop considerably following the L78 Turbo-Jet's release that spring, then picked up again during the last month of the 1965 run, ending in a final sales tally of 5,011.

Chevrolet's other new Corvette engine for 1965 offered much of the L76's might without the fuss and muss of solid lifters. Featuring a slightly milder hydraulic cam, the 350hp L79 327 produced its maximum power at a more usable 5800rpm as compared to the L76's 365hp at 6200rpm. The L79 was identical to the L76 on the outside with its chromed, round air cleaner and cast-aluminum, finned valve covers. Holley four-barrels and 11:1 compression were also shared by the two optional small blocks. The most noticeable differences were on the sticker, where the $107.60 L79 was $21.55 cheaper, and on the street, where the 350hp 327 was much more civilized while still possessing more than enough brute force to keep sports car rivals at bay.

Like Jerry Titus in reference to the 396, *Car and Driver*'s crew could barely believe their eyes. "A new engine for the Corvette? With hydraulic lifters? Three hundred-and-fifty horsepower at 5800rpm? Silky-smooth? No rough idle? No pushrod clatter? One hundred more horsepower than the [Ferrari] 250/GT? Sixty-eight more than the Aston-Martin [DB-5]?" After turning in an impressive 6.2 second 0-60 run and a 14.9 second 94mph quarter-mile pass for an L79 Sting Ray—a car they also lauded for its "outstanding" four-wheel discs, "stable" four-wheel independent suspension, and "silent" sophistication—*Car and Driver*'s testers were still scratching their heads. "You aren't suggesting that it's one of the best GT cars in

speed and G81 Positraction differential were mandatory with RPO L78.

As for chassis and drivetrain modifications, a revised frame cross-member was needed to mount the big-block in place of the more comfortable 327 small-blocks, as were stiffer front springs. Clutch diameter, at 10.4in, remained the same, but plate pressure was increased to handle all that Turbo-Jet torque. Beefed up as well were the rear halfshafts and U-joints, each being made of high-strength 4240 alloy steel and shot-peened to fight fatigue. Also added was a thicker 0.875in stabilizer bar (compared to the standard 0.750in bar) up front, while a new 0.562in sway bar was bolted on in back to help counteract the newfound under-

steer effects created by all that extra weight planted on the front wheels.

All told, the 396 big-block weighed about 680lb, easily 100lb more than its 327ci little brother. To Duntov's dismay, substituting Turbo-Jet power into the Sting Ray equation equaled an inherent forward weight bias. Wearing about 150 additional pounds—most coming at the nose—compared to its small-block brethren, a 1965 396 Corvette's front-to-rear weight distribution was 51/49; nothing frightening, mind you, but a marked departure from the direction Duntov had long envisioned for America's only sports car.

In all, six V-8s were available to Sting Ray buyers that year, with the standard the world, or are you?" Only L79 Corvette owners knew for sure.

Most major questions concerning the L78 big-block Corvette's place on this planet were answered almost immediately. According to Titus, "it goes like the proverbial scalded cat, will be cheaper than an injected 327 model, and has all the attributes of the normal Sting Ray to boot: quietness, weather-proofing, and comfort." Compared to the L84 fuelie's intimidating $538 asking price, the $292.70 L78 power option certainly appeared cheap. And when you consider what that option did for Sting Ray straight-line performance, the deal couldn't be beat.

Road & Track's stopwatch punchers had seen few cars like it. "Easing off the line with a chirp and then being careful to keep the tires just this side of broken loose gave us a 14.1 [quarter-mile time in seconds]," read *R&T*'s August 1965 review. "This is quick. Quicker than any other standard production car we've ever tested except the AC Cobra. Quick enough that nobody is likely to give you much trouble getting away from a stoplight. Except the law, maybe." But as impressed as they were over its newfound muscle, *Road & Track*'s editors couldn't help but question the Corvette's redirected approach to performance.

"It is difficult to describe precisely the 425bhp Corvette's place in the automotive scheme of things," continued *Road & Track*. "It's an interesting technical exercise, building a nice big engine like the 396 and putting it in a good chassis like the Corvette, but it honestly isn't a very satisfactory car for driving in everyday traffic. It's too much of a brute for that. And with all that power, any manner in which it is driven on anything except dead dry paving, the car is going to be a very large handful. It is not a car for the inexpert or the inattentive—two blinks of the eye and a careless poke of the toe and you could be in serious trouble." Contrary to other press claims that ride and handling weren't harmed to any substantial degree by the presence of all that cast-iron up front, Corvette engineer and racer Jerry Thompson minced few words when he later referred to the first big-block Sting Rays as "real cows."

Earlier, before RPO L78 was introduced, *Road & Track* had openly questioned the need for Chevrolet's Corvette to chase Shelby's Cobra in a cubic-inch battle it could never win. In their December 1964 edition, *R&T*'s reporters claimed that "though 400–425bhp is certainly going to propel the [Sting Ray] along at even higher rates of speed than the present 375, we're not at all certain that more horsepower is the answer so far as competition is concerned. The Corvette is simply too far overweight when it comes to competition like factory Cobras." Nonetheless, *Sports Car Graphic*'s Jerry Titus was still rooting on the Corvette-Cobra war in the March 1965 issue: "The big question, 'Will [the 396 Corvette] beat the 427 Cobra?' is a long way from answered yet."

Setting Titus' big question aside for the moment, *Road & Track* followed up with a plea of sorts for a return to sanity. "The proper approach, we think, is to make the most efficient use of a good design—which is what the fuel-injected 327 did—not simply to stuff in a bigger, stronger engine. There are many sports cars that honestly need more power. But the Corvette isn't one of them." Regardless of what *R&T* editors thought, or Duntov for that matter, more power would be on the way in the form of an even bigger Sting Ray big-block in 1966.

Small-block/big-block arguments notwithstanding, *Road & Track* did have a long list of good words for the 1965 Corvette. *R&T* especially liked the car's heater, which was "almost alone among sports cars in that it really works—even in cold weather." And in the magazine's words, the Muncie four-speed was "about as near faultless as any we've ever encountered."

As in previous years, 3.36:1 gears and a three-speed manual were standard for 1965, behind the equally rare base 250 and predominant L75 300hp 327s. And again, the optional Powerglide was available for these two small-blocks only, as was the wide-ratio M20 four-speed. Like the L78 big-block, the 365hp L76, 350hp L79, and 375hp L84 small-blocks were delivered with the close-ratio Muncie gearbox and 3.70:1 rear gears. Optional axle ratios once more included 3.08:1 highway cogs, 4.11:1 street-racers, and 4.56:1 drag-strip specials. A super heavy-duty Muncie four-speed, the soon-to-be-legendary M22 Rock Crusher, was also planned for 1965 production but didn't make the lineup.

Appearing prominently, on the other hand, was a finer fiberglass form, at least according to *Car Life*, which concluded that the 1965 Corvette "has improved somewhat in the quality of its finish. It seems that each year the characteristic ripples of the panels get a little less noticeable." Noted Corvette restoration expert Noland Adams agrees, explaining in his excellent *Corvette Restoration & Technical Guide, Volume 2* that "competition between [A. O. Smith and the St. Louis assembly plant] resulted in continuous improvements in Corvette body fit and finish. Although 1963–67 Corvette body quality was probably at its highest in 1966, 1965 was certainly a good year."

Hands down, it was a great year as far as the fiberglass-wrapped package as a whole was concerned. As in 1963 and 1964, Sting Ray production for 1965 set another record, this time reaching 23,562: 15,376 convertibles and 8,186 coupes. The 1965 Corvette remained simply irresistible. Continued *Car Life*, its "combination of ride and handling is unchallenged among American cars and right up with the best production sports cars made anywhere. It goes, it stops, it handles, and it does all in comfort, silence and reliability. And, above all else, it's great fun to drive. There's just nothing quite like it at within $1000 of its price."

Motor Trend's Bob McVay couldn't have agreed more. "Unique on the Detroit scene," he wrote in the April 1965 issue, "that's still Chevrolet's Corvette Sting Ray. It's as yet the only true American sports car. It makes no concessions for carrying more than two people and a reasonable amount of luggage, and it doesn't claim to be anything except what it is. What is the Corvette? It's one of the hottest performing, best handling, most comfortable sports cars on the market, and some think it's one of the best looking as well. Each year since its 1953 introduction, the 'Vette has been getting more refined, faster, better handling, and gentler riding. In standard form, Corvette's 1965 offerings are smooth, quiet, comfortable sports cars, capable of staggering performance depending on what engine you order. A better all-around sports car would be hard to find at any price. We loved it."

No kidding.

Chapter Six

1966

Building a Bigger, Better Big-Block

When the so-called Mystery Motor first appeared at Daytona in February 1963 its displacement measured 427ci, thanks to a 4.25in bore and 3.76in stroke. Two years later, when Chevrolet engineers finally decided to re-introduce their porcupine powerplant for street duty, the resulting Mark IV big-block displaced 396ci due to a slight bore reduction made to allow the new Turbo-Jet V-8 authorized entry into Chevy's second-edition mid-sized Chevelle. Late in 1964, the killjoys at General Motors had established a 400ci maximum displacement limit for its divisions' intermediates in an attempt to keep a lid on performance passions, which at the time were just starting to boil again after GM officials had supposedly cooled things off with their infamous anti-racing edict of January 1963.

There were, however, no such limits at the top of Chevrolet's performance ladder, where the 1965 Sting Ray had made do with the 396ci version of the Mark IV V-8. No one complained, though, since the 396 Turbo-Jet's 425 horses stood ready, willing, and able to make Chevy's first big-block Corvette the meanest, nastiest American performance machine this side of Shelby-American's uncivilized 427 Cobra. But if curbside critics thought the 1965 396 Corvette was wild, they had another thing coming—and it arrived in 1966, when Zora Duntov's Sting Ray joined Carroll Shelby's Cobra atop the sports car realm's cubic-inch leader board.

The transition from 396 Turbo-Jet to 427 Turbo-Jet was as simple as boring the Mark IV cylinder block to match to its Mark II roots. As Duntov told *Car and Driver* in the fall of 1965, "this was done primarily to save weight. You must remember that cast iron is very heavy, and by removing 30 cubic inches of it we have made a significant reduction in weight." Of course Zora was kidding, but there was nothing funny about the Corvette's 427, a brutal big-block that owed nothing to any other regular-production powerplant on the planet.

"Unless you're wheelin' a 'street hemi' or a 427 Cobra," warned *Cars* magazine's Martyn Schorr, "steer clear of Chevy's hottest street stinger." The 427 Corvette can "literally walk away and hide from any domestic production car, except for the Shelby 427 Cobra and MoPar street hemi. Even though Chevrolet insists on being divorced from anything that even hints of racing the 1966 Sting Ray can be ordered with a fantastic amount of genuine racing equipment."

Available in two forms, the optional 427 Turbo-Jet V-8 topped off that equipment list in high-powered fashion. Buyers who wanted a big, bad Turbo-Jet that

Base price for a 1966 Corvette convertible was $4,084. Production was 17,762. Sales of the options appearing here were 3,617 for the $131.65 N14 sidemount exhausts, 1,194 for the $316 P48 Kelsey-Hayes knock-off wheels, and 5,557 for the $46.55 T01 goldwall tires. Notice the incorrect bright center cones (behind the knock-off spinners) on these P48 wheels. Corvettes knock-offs in 1964 and 1965 had chrome-plated cones, while 1966 P48 wheels used brushed-finish cones (see the Sunfire Yellow 1966 coupe shown in this chapter).

A 1966 small-block Corvette rolls down the St. Louis assembly line, followed by two big-blocks and another small-block in the distance.

didn't have a big, bad attitude could check off RPO L36, priced at $181.20. Based on a Mark IV cylinder block with two-bolt main bearing caps, the L36 427 featured domesticated hydraulic lifters, reasonably mild 10.25:1 compression, cast-aluminum pistons, and a hefty Holley four-barrel on a cast-iron intake manifold. Intake valves, at 2.06in, were smaller than those used in the 1965 L78 396, and

valve lift (0.461in intake, 0.480in exhaust) was down as well. Maximum output for the L36 big-block was originally listed as 400hp at 5400rpm, then was almost immediately lowered to 390hp at 5200rpm. Maximum torque was a whopping 460lb-ft at 3600rpm.

Chevrolet's other 427 Turbo-Jet cost quite a bit more, and for good reason. Priced at $312.85, RPO L72 started with a cylinder block held together on the bottom end by four-bolt main bearing caps. Like its smaller L78 predecessor, the L72 427 was stuffed full of 11:1 impact-extruded aluminum pistons and a lumpy

solid-lifter cam. The L78's mechanical cam certainly had been no wimp in 1965, but the L72's 0.519in lift unit made it look weak in comparison. Mandatory K66 transistorized ignition, a 780cfm Holley four-barrel on an aluminum intake, and free-flowing exhaust manifolds completed the L72 package, a burly power source that was even more mighty than its 396ci Mark IV forerunner. Just as the L36 was first rated at 400hp, L72 output was originally listed as 450hp at 6400rpm, then quickly adjusted down, in this case to 425hp at 5600rpm. Top torque was identical to the L36's rating, but came on 400rpm higher.

No specific explanation for those horsepower adjustments exists, though it's not difficult to guess why they happened considering the long-running battle between Chevrolet's performance planners and GM's anti-racing faction, the latter group especially conscious of the federal government's growing concern over automotive safety. Someone high up surely must have stepped in, once Duntov's engineers started playing with more than 400 horses. At the time, GM was preparing to institute yet another power-restricting rule-of-thumb, this one limiting passenger cars to no less than ten pounds of curb weight per one advertised horsepower, although again, this limit didn't apply to America's only sports car. Nonetheless, 450hp in an automobile that weighed only 3,300lb was asking for a bit too much leeway from the brass on the fourteenth floor. Lowering that red flag, on the other hand, was as easy as pulling out an eraser and writing in a less threatening advertised figure. A new decal on the L72's chrome air cleaner and it was back to business as usual. Few, however, were fooled.

Among others, *Motor Trend* noted the change, then took a shot at answering why. "One explanation for this curious state of affairs making the rounds is that, since the congressional safety inquisition, there has been a gentlemen's agreement among parties concerned not to advertise more than 425hp. No official explanations have been offered [for the L72's drop from 450hp], and Chevrolet's sticking to the 425hp figure in its latest literature. A similar situation is said to exist at Ford and Chrysler, too, whose high-performance engines are believed capable of gross power ratings far in excess of the 425hp they each claim."

Anyone who believed Chevy's 425hp claim needed only to drop the hammer once on an L72 Corvette. As *Car and Driver*'s road testers reported, "Chevrolet insists that there are only 425 horses in there, and we'll just have to take their word for it. Though we feel compelled to point out that these are 425 horses of a size and strength never before seen by man—horses as tall as houses, with hooves as big as bushel baskets. When you have *this* many of *those* horses exerting their full force against the small of

your back, you are profoundly impressed, and you will most likely lose all interest in counting anyway."

Motor Trend's Bob McVay was equally skeptical. Chevrolet "coyly rates [the L72] at 425hp," he wrote in the March 1966 issue, "but we think an extra two teams of Borax mules lie hidden behind the barn door. Engineers call it 'porcupine,' but that refers to the valve layout and not its agility." McVay's test of a 425hp 1966 Corvette convertible with optional 4.11:1 rear gears produced some sizzling results: 0-60mph in 5.6 ticks, and the quarter-mile in 13.4sec at 105mph. Top speed at the 6500rpm redline was listed as 135mph.

All numbers—advertised or whatever—aside, McVay simply couldn't say enough about the L72's raw-boned muscle. In his words, "the 427 has the kind of torque that made World War II fighter planes try to wrap themselves around their propeller on take-off. In the relatively light, front-end-heavy Corvette this verve tends to pave the highway with your rear-tire treads." Echoed *Car and Driver*, "there's power literally everywhere, great gobs of steam-locomotive, earth-moving torque."

Doing McVay one better, *Sports Car Graphic*'s Jerry Titus reported an even more impressive 0-60mph time of 4.8sec for an L72 coupe also fitted with a 4.11:1

Corvettes received yet another distinctive, restyled, standard simulated knock-off wheel cover for 1966.

differential. "The porcupine engine—which first saw the light of day as a 427, not a 396—is a beaut," wrote Titus. "There's gobs of low end torque and a willingness to grab revs that belies its size. It'll turn seven grand, so the 6500 redline is conservative. Tell us you'd like a hotter performing road machine than this and we'll call you some kinda nut!"

Perhaps most amazing was *Car and Driver*'s' test of an L72 convertible sporting somewhat mild 3.36:1 cogs. "With the normal 3.36 rear axle ratio it'll turn a quarter mile that'll give a GTO morning sickness, and still run a top speed of around 150mph," claimed a report in the magazine's November 1965 issue. Rest to 60mph took only 5.4sec, according to that report, while the quarter-mile's far end arrived in a sensational 12.8sec, with trap speeds hitting 112mph. The 425hp Sting Ray "accelerates from zero to 100 in less than eleven seconds," continued *Car and Driver*, "and is so smooth and controllable in the three-figure speed ranges that it all becomes sort of unreal."

In that same issue, *Car and Driver* also thrashed one of Shelby-American's Ford-powered 427 Cobras, proving that physical laws simply can never be broken. Weighing a mere 2,890lb—a quarter-ton less than the L72 Sting Ray convertible— the 425hp Cobra seared the track to the

A new egg-crate grille and "Corvette Sting Ray" script added to the hood represented the quickest way to identify the mildly revamped 1966 model. New exterior colors for 1966 included Laguna Blue, Trophy Blue, Mosport Green, and Sunfire Yellow, joining Tuxedo Black, Ermine White, Rally Red, Nassau Blue, Silver Pearl, and Milano Maroon.

tune of 12.2sec at 118mph in the quarter-mile, and 4.3sec for the time-honored 0–60mph run. Most alarming was the Cobra's ability to hit 100mph *and* return to rest in a scant 14.5sec. Clearly Duntov's engineering crew could have done themselves a favor by setting their sights lower, perhaps in the direction of Shelby-American's other Ford-powered sportster, the GT-350 Mustang. As it was, Shelby's super-quick snake would become extinct within a year anyway, leaving the GT-350, and its soon-to-be-announced GT-

500 big-block brother, to carry on the battle with Chevrolet's fiberglass two-seater. It came by default, but the tables finally would be turned on Shelby in 1967, at least on the street.

As for the 1966 427 Corvette, like the 396 Sting Ray the previous year, it featured a strong supporting cast including that same bulging hood. Suspension was beefed and a 0.562in rear antisway bar was incorporated. Standard transmission fare was the wide-ratio M20 four-speed (2.56:1 low) for the 390hp L36, while the

In 1965, there had been five 327 small-block V-8s available to Corvette buyers. In 1966, there were only two as the yeoman 250hp 327 and solid-lifter 365hp L76 were dropped, leaving the 300hp 327 as the base Sting Ray powerplant, while this 350hp L79 (missing its air cleaner decal) remained as the one optional small-block. Air conditioning, RPO C60, was priced at $412.90 in 1966. RPO C60 production was 3,520.

Left
Options appearing here on this 1966 convertible include air conditioning (C60), AM/FM radio (U69), the teakwood steering wheel (N32), Powerglide (M35), leather seats, and the telescopic steering wheel (N36). The telescopic wheel ($42.15) was adjusted through a three-inch range by the finned-locking nut located between the horn button and steering wheel center. Leather seats cost $79, the teakwood wheel $47.40, $199.10 bought the U69 radio, and Powerglide was a $194.85 option.

The Door to Recognition

Although the same basic Sting Ray shell carried over from 1963 to 1967, differentiating one model from the next is not particularly difficult, as long as you knew where to look. Rocker moldings and wheel covers changed every year, various grilles and fender louvers were used, and of course you couldn't miss a 1963 coupe with its twin hood grilles and that trademark rear "stinger." Another identifying feature was the fuel filler door, which received a distinctive treatment each model year. Study these photos carefully, you will be tested.

1964

1966

1963

1965

1967

425hp L72 was mated to the close-ratio Muncie (2.20:1 low), which became an option in itself, RPO M21, for 1966. The milder L36 could also be backed by the M35 Powerglide automatic, although only twenty buyers made that choice. Equally rare was the new M22 heavy-duty Muncie four-speed, available for the L72 only.

Rumors of a special, bulletproof gearbox had been floating around since early 1965. More than one press report at the time hinted at a wide array of purpose-built, SCCA-legal racing components to come, including such prominent pieces as aluminum heads and a stout four-speed capable of handling more than 500hp. But none of these parts appeared for 1965, though RPO M22 was planned for production that year. When it did appear in 1966, the M22 four-speed was aptly named Rock Crusher due to its noisy operation. Inside, an M22 differed from its M20 and M21 brethren by using beefier gears with heavier teeth cut at a lesser angle—it was the gnashing of these teeth that inspired the Rocker Crusher's name. Externally, all three Muncie boxes were quite similar. Compared to the 13,903 M21s and 10,837 M20s sold, both costing $184.35, only fifteen L72 buyers spent another $237 for RPO M22.

Chevrolet also introduced a new, stronger, fully synchronized Saginaw three-speed manual transmission as standard equipment for the base 300hp 327 small-block (the 250hp 327 was dropped after 1965) in 1966. Both the M20 four-speed and Powerglide automatic were available behind the base 327. Backing up the fourth engine in the 1966 Corvette lineup—the 350hp L79 327—was either the M20 or M21 Muncie four-speed. Neither the standard three-speed nor the optional Powerglide could be ordered with RPO L79.

Standard gear ratio for the L72 427 was 3.55:1, with additional choices including the aforementioned 3.36:1 and 4.11:1 axles, joined by a 3.70:1 unit. M20-equipped L36 427s came with 3.08 gears, while an M21 or M35 Powerglide behind a 390hp big-block meant a 3.36:1 differential was in back.

Among returning popular performance pieces were both the $36.90 N11 off-road exhausts and the more noticeable N14 side-mounts, the latter option dropping in price to $131.65 as demand

Just starting it makes your stomach muscles tighten

Buckle into that businesslike Corvette seat. Turn the key. Rowrow row . . . BhruUM!

And it happens. The blend of husky, eager noises you expect from a car like the Sting Ray.

That insistent throb is the Turbo-Jet 427 you ordered, 425 horsepower churning under the domed hood.

You sense great gulps of air rushing down through a four-barrel carburetor to their final explosion

while unshrouded valves, solid lifters and a special cam do their stuff.

Now, wipe your perspiring palm and slip that gear box into first cog. Snick! You're about to have a driving experience you'll remember

Corvette . . . Excitement the Chevrolet Way

Rest to 60mph in less than 5sec. Seeing the far end of a quarter-mile in about 12.8 ticks of the clock. This type of performance would've tightened more than your stomach muscles.

naturally picked up. Offered alongside all four engines, the loud, sexy sidepipes were selected by 3,617 Corvette customers in 1966. Less common, undoubtedly due to their still heavy $316 asking price, the P48 Kelsey-Hayes aluminum

knock-off wheels remained suitable complements for the N14 exhausts. RPO P48 sales totaled 1,194.

Coupe buyers could still opt for the big 36.5gal tank (sixty-six did), while all customers choosing the three optional

powerplants were also able to add the K66 transistorized ignition. Leather seats, tinted glass, power brakes, steering, and windows, telescopic steering column, teakwood steering wheel, air condition-

Left
The crossflags on the fender meant one of the two small-block V-8s was beneath the hood; in this case it's the standard 300hp 327. Notice that the familiar red, white, and blue markings on these P48 knock-off spinners have long-since faded from this basically original, one-owner 1966 coupe, a car that has seen its fair share of both daily driving and long-distance touring. Gone as well is the original rubber, replaced by modern radials. Standard equipment included either Goodyear or Firestone two-ply nylon cord tires. Available at extra cost were the P92 rayon whitewalls and T01 goldwall nylon tires.

ing, removable hardtop—all the familiar comfort and convenience pieces were present and accounted for. New attractions included bucket seat headrests (RPO A82), shoulder harnesses (A85), and four-way hazard warning lights (V74), the last feature coming in response to the growing number of states requiring cars to have some form of onboard traffic warning system. A sign of things to come also appeared in the form of an air-injection reactor made mandatory for the first time in 1966 on all Corvettes (except L72 models) delivered in California and listed as RPO K19 for Sting Rays sold elsewhere.

Last, but certainly not least among the group of new options for 1966 were two packages bound to put a twinkle in the eye of those continually winking at

Base priced at $4,295, the 1966 Corvette coupe again was outsold by its topless counterpart by a wide margin: 17,762 to 9,958. Notice the backup lights; both this feature and the day/night rearview mirror, items offered in 1965 as part of the optional Comfort and Convenience group (RPO Z01), became standard equipment in 1966. Alert readers may have already noticed the Rally Red 1966 convertible shown in this chapter does not have the correct backup lenses. The trailer hitch appearing here is an owner-installed item.

the commonly held notion that "Chevrolet wasn't in racing." The first, RPO J56, was a familiar code, having been present in 1964 for buyers who had wanted the best brakes possible. The second, RPO F41, would kick off a Chevrolet tradition

RPO N32 featured a classy teakwood rim glued and fitted to the typical steel three-spoke wheel. Also notice the tachometer with its "mild" redline, meaning this small-block coupe has the base 300hp 327. Adding the optional 350hp L76 in 1966 automatically included a tach with a 6000rpm redline.

of exceptional sport suspension setups that still survives today. Together, the two were unbeatable.

Of course, standard brakes were still the excellent Delco four-wheel 11.75in discs, equipment that inspired *Cars'* Martyn Schorr to call the 1966 427 Sting Ray the "quickest, fastest, stoppingest 'Vette yet!" Even during the roughest street play these super binders were up to the task, but inhumanly harsh use could bring out their mortal side, however briefly. As *Car Life* explained, "only when we made a series of consecutive stops from 120mph

did demon fade rear his smelly head." Everything, even Corvette's excellent four-wheel disc setup, has its limits.

Big-block Corvette customers who wanted to push those limits in 1966 could have shelled out an extra $342.30 for the new J56 disc brakes. Like its 1964 drum-brake predecessor, the 1966 J56 heavy-duty disc option included metallic linings. Compared to standard discs (with organic linings), these semi-metallic pads were larger and were bonded, not riveted, to beefier nickel-alloy backing plates held in place by two retaining pins instead of one. Each front caliper was also reinforced by an iron brace, and a proportioning valve was included to help balance braking pressure between front and rear wheels. Completing the J56 package was the J50 power booster and dual-circuit master cylinder—standard brakes were energized by a single-chamber master cylinder. Perhaps because of its price,

perhaps because it represented more brakes than the average Corvette driver would ever use, sales of the J56 option totaled only 382 units.

Another 427-exclusive option, RPO F41, replaced the 1965 F40 option and apparently was offered only with the 425hp L72 big-block (once again, 327 and L36 equipped 1966 Corvettes with F41 are known) at a humble price of $36.90. F41 features included heavier, nonvariable-rate springs front and rear, stiffer shocks, and a 0.94in front sway bar. F41 production was 2,705.

Already appropriately beefed up, an L72 Corvette's standard suspension worked well enough on its own in many critics' eyes, although anyone who had come to appreciate the truly agile 327 Sting Ray in top trim knew that most compliments aimed at the big-block Corvette's ride and handling were made with many obvious qualifications left un-

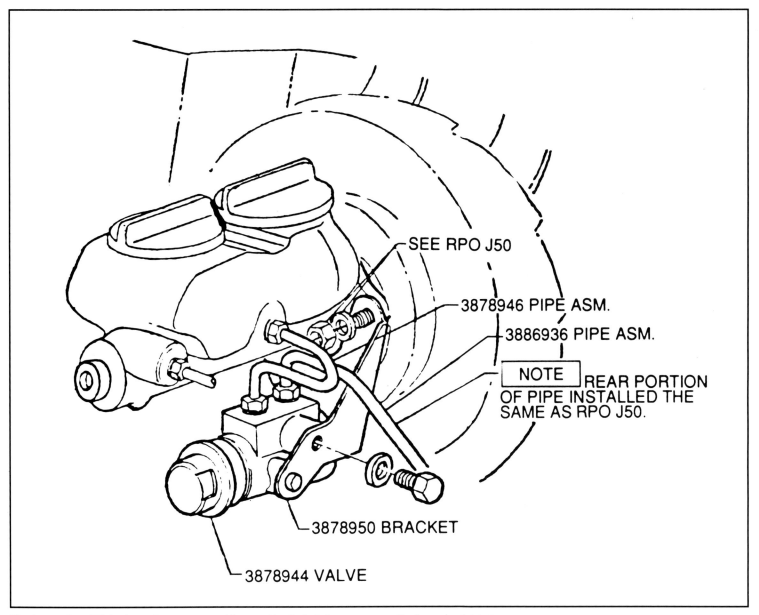

SEE RPO J50

3878946 PIPE ASM.

3886936 PIPE ASM.

NOTE REAR PORTION OF PIPE INSTALLED THE SAME AS RPO J50.

3878950 BRACKET

3878944 VALVE

The heavy-duty J56 brake option reappeared for 1966, adding power assist, metallic linings, and special beefed-up brake pad retainers up front. Also included was a proportioning valve (at bottom) that allowed the driver to adjust the balance between front and rear braking power.

Previous pages
Two 427ci big-blocks replaced the 425hp 396 Turbo-Jet as the top Corvette power option for 1966. RPO L36, the 390hp 427, was priced at $181.20, while the meaner 425hp L72 427 cost a healthy $312.85. This Mosport Green L72 Sting Ray is one of 5,258—coupe and convertible—built in 1966. Another 5,116 L36 big-block 1966 Corvettes were also produced. Like the Rally Red convertible appearing in this chapter, this 1966 427 Corvette also has the bright knock-off wheel center cones instead of the proper brushed-finish pieces.

Above
Anyone who drove a 1966 L72 Corvette questioned that 425hp rating, and Chevrolet didn't help matters by initially advertising this big-block at 450 horses. As Motor Trend's Bob McVay wrote, "for drivers who have the guts and skill to master it—and the maturity to recognize it for what it is and handle it accordingly—the 427

Turbo-Jet Corvette is a road king. The other 99 percent of the population is likely to be much happier and safer in either of the two 327 models." In conclusion, McVay reiterated his position, explaining that "for those rare individuals who want and can handle, its potential, the 427 Turbo-Jet is a red-hot machine, but if it gets away from you, don't say we didn't warn you."

said. Simply put, heavy and nimble rarely go hand in hand. But regardless of physical laws, most reviews of the big-block chassis were on the positive side. According to *Car and Driver*, "the extra weight of this big engine doesn't really seem to affect the car's handling at all. There's a general feeling of ponderousness that one associates with any of the bigger sports machines at low speeds, but when you're going fast it's quick and responsive."

Describing the F41 ride was a slightly different call, as Jerry Titus discovered during his test of an L72 coupe. "With the optional suspension," he began in *Sports Car Graphic*'s December 1965 issue, "the ride is very firm, pleasant enough for smooth roads, but almost uncomfortable on bumpy, wavy surfaces." Bumpy or not, Titus' ride still left him impressed with the compromise made between pleasure and performance. "We logged almost 350 miles in one day covering all kinds of roads," continued Titus, "and neither driver nor passenger felt any overall discomfort. As a matter of fact, the firmness represented security as the right foot kept getting heavier and heavier."

With all the attention given prominent new features like the F41 suspension, J56 brakes, and the big, beautiful 427s, basic model upgrades were lost in the shuffle, a result by no means undeserved. Basic exterior changes for 1966 again were limited to different rocker moldings, restyled wheel covers, and a redesigned grille, this one an attractive egg-crate design. Less noticeable trim adjustments included adding the familiar "Corvette Sting Ray" script to the hood's leading corner on the driver's side. And Chevrolet finally gave up entirely on the roof vents behind the doors, deleting them along with the electric interior ventilation system used, albeit weakly, in 1964 and 1965. Another resewn bucket seat style with additional horizontal pleats, a vinyl-covered foam headliner in place of the previously used fiberboard, chrome door-pull handles, and standard backup lights were also new for 1966.

Overall, Chevrolet offered Corvette buyers in 1966 the best of both worlds with two polite small-block models and two big-block bullies. Among the former, the 350hp L79 Sting Ray was still the same car that had *Car and Driver* comparing it in 1965 to some of Europe's best. In

To be specific, the price for a 425hp coupe in 1966 was more than $4,500, and could crowd $5,000 in a hurry if a buyer found himself unable to resist the wide array of optional teasers.

the upper ranks, the 390hp L36 427 Corvette was a relatively affordable way for a driver to enter Chevrolet's super-car fraternity without all the fuss and muss commonly associated with the all-out Mark IV motors. The two bookends, the 300hp standard Sting Ray and the outrageous 425hp L72 screamer, were as different as night and day. But all were Corvettes, and Corvettes still stood at the top of Detroit's ever-changing pecking order as far as class, luxury, pizzazz, and performance were concerned.

It just didn't get any better.

Chapter Seven

1967

Unintended Encore

Once the all-new Sting Ray hit the streets in the fall of 1962 Chevrolet couldn't build them fast enough, not even after putting on an extra shift at the St. Louis assembly plant. Corvette model-year sales jumped by 50 percent in 1963, reaching an all-time high of 21,513 cars. Convertible sales alone that year missed topping the entire 1961 total by only 20 units. And if that wasn't good news enough for Chevrolet's bean counters, Sting Ray sales continued upward each year: 22,229 in 1964, 23,562 in 1965, and a healthy 27,720 in 1966. As a sidelight, after predicting in 1963 that the new coupe would end up dominating future sales, those same product planners watched as topless Corvettes slowly gained momentum, then completely overwhelmed their fastback running mates. Following a near even split in 1963, the coupe's share of the market dropped to 37.3 percent in 1964 and stayed near that level until 1969.

Clearly, William Mitchell and Zora Arkus-Duntov knew a little about what they were doing while overseeing the creation of the all-new Corvette. The sporty, sexy 1963 Sting Ray certainly was deserving of every rave and more. But resting on laurels represents the easiest way to miss the bus in Detroit, where today's news ends up old news almost as soon as it's fit to print. Working three to four, sometimes five years in advance has long been the norm when it comes to building new cars; by the time that new machine is turning heads on Mainstreet USA, the next edition is already well under way.

Timeless classic or not, the Sting Ray was no exception. Even as thrilled buyers were flocking by the proverbial droves to their nearest Corvette dealer in late 1962, Bill Mitchell was busy dreaming up another exciting, all-new look for America's only true sports car, an image all at Chevrolet hoped would wow the masses again in 1967. By the spring of 1965, Mitchell had his next new look in the form of Larry Shinoda's Mako Shark show car, a long, low, sleek concoction with bulging wheelhouses at all four corners. Initially a non-running mockup, Shinoda's Mako Shark soon became the Mako Shark II once it was decided to rename the XP-755 Shark of 1961 the Mako Shark I. Later in the year, work began on a fully functional Mako Shark II using the new Mark IV big-block V-8.

At the same time, Duntov was back working on his mid-engined dream Corvette, an effort that once again would prove fruitless. Much closer to reality was the project then under way in stylist Henry Haga's studio under the direction of

This 1967 roadster is equipped with the L71 435hp 427. It also sports the N14 sidemount exhausts, priced at $131.65, and the redesigned bolt-on cast-aluminum wheels, RPO N89. Only 720 buyers shelled out $263.30 in 1967 for the N89 wheels. Production of L71 Corvettes, coupes and convertibles, was 3,754.

Larry Shinoda's Mako Shark II was designed in 1965 as the inspiration for the next new Corvette, which was initially planned for 1967. Developmental difficulties eventually delayed that debut until 1968, meaning the so-called "midyear" Sting Ray body had to run one extra year.

Chevrolet chief stylist David Holls. Using Shinoda's Mako Shark II image as a base, Haga's studio had created the next new Corvette's shell midway through 1965, with a working prototype running under test at the Milford Proving Grounds that fall.

Track tests, however, showed the new model suffered from high-speed lift characteristics, and Duntov didn't like the way those bulging corners inhibited visibility. Both these negatives could be fixed, but not within what little time was left between that point and the planned 1967 new-model introduction. So it was back to the drawing board for Haga and Shinoda's 1967 Corvette, a more-than-modern-looking machine that then became Chevrolet's 1968 Corvette.

Stylists were left with no choice but to dress up the old familiar Sting Ray for one more encore, after they thought they'd already done that job in 1966. While it very well could have ended up a rubber-stamp effort, the resulting 1967 makeover emerged as perhaps the best of the breed in the opinion of many fiberglass fans, both then and now.

Car and Driver subscribers liked the 1967 Corvette so much they voted it the Best All-Around Car for 1967, a first for Chevrolet's performance machine, which also copped Best GT and Best Sports Car over 3000cc that year in *Car and Driver's* annual readers' poll. "As it sits, the Sting Ray is the most sophisticated passenger car made in America—in terms of engine, drivetrain, suspension and brakes—and among the best engineered sports cars made anywhere," claimed the May 1967 report. "If that isn't good enough to make it the Best All-Around Car of 1967, we'd like to know what is."

Road & Track's staff was also impressed: "The Sting Ray is in its fifth and probably last year with that name and body style, and it finally looks the way we thought it should have in the first place. All the funny business—the fake vents, extraneous emblems and simulated-something-or-other wheel covers—is gone, and though some consider the basic shape overstyled, it looks more like a finished product now."

All typically minor exterior changes were performed in the best interests of letting the pure Sting Ray form shine through. Engine identification, small-block or big-block, was stripped from the fenders, which became even cleaner with the addition of a smaller, more modern

louver arrangement that featured a slight forward rake. Accentuating those clean bodysides were new rocker moldings that were nearly completely blacked-out. Up front, the traditional crossflag emblem was smaller and the "Corvette" script used on the hood in 1966 was deleted.

If anything bordered on "funny business," it was the 1967 Sting Ray's bold big-block hood, although nearly all critics agreed the new "stinger" style nonfunctional scoop was both extremely attractive and a marked improvement over the somewhat crude big-block bulge used in 1965 and 1966. Not all big-block hoods hid big-block 427s in 1967, however, since a mishap involving molds for the flat small-block hood left St. Louis plant officials no choice but to assemble 327 Sting Rays with 427 hoods for a few days in late February or early March 1967. Dealers undoubtedly made the same swap themselves in response to customer

requests for that sexy scoop atop a small-block, a combination the St. Louis plant wouldn't perform under normal circumstances.

Along with that scoop, the 1967 big-block hood also received a set of paint stripes that either contrasted or complemented the exterior finish, depending on the interior trim. For example, a black Sting Ray with a black or red interior received red striping, while a black car with saddle or green appointments inside were adorned with a white scoop. In addition to the red and white stripes, hood scoops were also painted black, dark teal blue, or medium bright blue. Thanks to problems perfecting the painting process, some early 1967 427 Corvettes were delivered with no stripes at all.

Overall, paint and body quality earned high marks in 1967. Calling the 1967 Corvette's paint its "most arresting aspect," *Hot Rod*'s Eric Dahlquist claimed

Shown here is a prototype 1967 427 Corvette coupe. Notice the proposed three-bladed spinners on the wheels' hub caps, items that clashed somewhat with the "cleaned up" image applied to the last of the first-generation Sting Rays.

the finish "does a pretty good job at being smooth and free of orange peel." According to *Road & Track*, the 1967 Sting Ray's paint "was better than on any Corvette we've tested." *Motor Trend* writer Steve Kelly liked the general finish, explaining that "Chevrolet has had over 15 years to learn about working with fiberglass, and it shows in the almost flawless workmanship of the body." Dahlquist, however, disagreed, pointing out that "early Sting Rays endured a session of poor-fitting fiberglass components, a situation we thought had been put behind years ago but appears to crop up in places, like the way our doors failed

Many critics lauded the 1967 Corvette for its clean appearance as the so-called excess clutter, like the 1966 model's fender emblems and hood script, were deleted. The restyled functional fender louvers were also less obtrusive. Completing the package was a set of standard Rally wheels that were both attractive and helped cool the four-wheel disc brakes through the slots in the rims' center sections. Chevrolet built 8,504 coupes in 1967 offering them at a base price of $4,388.75.

to match the rear quarters by almost a 1/2-inch."

On the other hand, you had to go a long way to find a bad word about the new standard Corvette wheel introduced in 1967. Curbside hacks had continually taken pot shots at the somewhat overdone simulated mag-style wheel covers used in 1965 and 1966. The spinners previously mounted on all Sting Ray wheel covers since 1963 were also considered to

be a little too much by many. In contrast the 1967 Rally wheel was simple and stunning at the same time, its painted steel center section set off by chrome trim rings and an equally bright understated hubcap. Functional as well as attractive, the 15in Rally wheel featured brake-cooling slots and was a half-inch wider than the previous 15x5.5in standard steel rim.

Designers modified the optional cast-aluminum wheel as well, basically because

Standard Sting Ray power for 1967 again came from the 300hp 327, which 6,858 buyers opted for that year. Another 6,375 customers chose the other available small-block, the optional 350hp L79, priced at $105.35. Air conditioning, RPO C60, cost $412.90 and was installed on 3,788 1967 Sting Rays. Notice the dual-circuit master cylinder (directly above the chrome ignition shielding), a new standard brake feature in 1967.

Right
This Sunfire Yellow 1967 convertible is equipped with the 390hp L36 427—total 1967 L36 production, coupes and convertibles—was 3,832. Price for RPO L36 was $200.15.

they had to. Ever-growing federally mandated automotive safety standards in 1967 precluded the use of the Corvette's racing-inspired knock-off wheel, its adapter arrangement and three-pronged spinner deemed by government agencies as being

Zora Duntov grins as engineer Denny Davis dyno tests an L88 prototype (notice road draft tube on the right valve cover) in May 1966. This particu-lar version has iron cylinder heads; regular-pro-duction L88s used the aluminum heads also of-fered as RPO L89 for the street-legal L71 427.

Seatbelts got push-button releases and the buckets' backrests got positive latch-es. Four-way flashers, another 1966 op-tion, became standard in 1967 and the turn signal system was revised with a "freeway lane change" feature—a little pressure in the desired direction activated the signal, leaving the busy driver not to fret over clicking the lever fully in and out of place.

Also among interior revamps was an easier-to-use parking brake handle, relo-cated from beneath the dash to between the seats. Although it was practical and possessed a certain sporty flair, the new handbrake made it all but impossible to carry an extra stowaway passenger, an undesirable, yet sometimes performed practice of previous years. "This is good from an insurance company's point of view," wrote *Cars* magazine's Martyn Schorr, "but it further limits the already limited passenger space. Third passen-gers, especially females, will have to think a few times before accepting a ride in a 1967 Ray!"

Safety-conscious options again in-cluded shoulder harnesses, headrests, and tinted glass, items joined in 1967 by RPO U15, a speed-warning indicator incorpo-rated, somewhat paradoxically, into the 160mph speedometer. By turning a small knob in the speedo's center, the driver could preset a maximum mile-per-hour limit; once he surpassed that limit on his way around the dial a buzzer would re-mind him of his transgression, hopefully before a state trooper stepped in to do the honors himself. And for drivers con-scious of the safety of their removable hardtop's finish, a new vinyl covering, RPO C08, was available for an extra $52.70, on top of the C07 roof's $231.75 asking price.

Positraction continued as the over-whelming choice on the options list (89 percent of the buyers forked up $42.15 for RPO G81 in 1967), and the attractive side-mount exhausts remained popular as well. Still present among the RPO codes were the N11 off-road exhausts, K19 air injection reactor, J50 power brakes, J56 heavy-duty brakes, K66 transistorized ig-nition, F41 special suspension, and N03 oversized fuel tank, offered for the last time, and for good reason—only two N03 tanks were sold in 1967. Except for the discontinued teakwood steering

not fit for human consumption. Behind the 1967 N89 aluminum wheel's simple Bow-Tie center cap were the typical five lugs found on conventional wheels. Even though the "romance" of the knock-offs was lost, the new wheel finally did its weight-saving thing like an aluminum wheel should—in previous years, any pounds trimmed by the addition of RPO P48 were offset by the adapter equipment required to convert from the standard five-lug mounting setup to the quick-change knock-off design.

Safety concerns also helped inspire a long list of additional new standard Corvette features for 1967. Under the hood, a dual-circuit master cylinder—op-tional with J50 power assist and the J56

heavy-duty brake package in 1966—re-placed the previously used single-cham-ber brake cylinder. Included as well was a malfunction warning system that in-formed the driver of his potential demise by flashing a red light on the instrument panel.

Inside, both that panel and the steer-ing column were redesigned with energy-absorbing characteristics. A thicker lip was added to the foam dash pad, and the shatter-resistant day/night mirror got a vinyl-padded frame and breakaway sup-port. Dashboard knobs were mushroom-faced, and window regulator knobs were plastic, while the door handles themselves free wheeled, meaning they were ren-dered inoperative once the locks were set.

wheel, all extra-cost comfort and convenience features were carryovers from 1966.

Quite different, though, was the 1967 powertrain lineup. Things remained unchanged at the bottom of the list, where the base 300hp 327 and optional 350hp L79 small-block soldiered on. Familiar as well was the L36 427 big-block with its hydraulic lifters, single Holley four-barrel, and 390 horses at the ready. Again, the Saginaw three-speed manual transmission was standard behind the 300hp small-block, with the M20 wide-ratio Muncie four-speed and M35 Powerglide still around on the options list. L79 327 buyers could pick between the M20 and M21 close-ratio four-speed, as could L36 customers, who could also select the Powerglide automatic if shiftless big-block performance was desired. Once more, Powerglide was not available behind the 350hp small-block.

From there, the powertrain pecking order was revamped considerably thanks to the appearance of three little Holley two-barrel carburetors. Triple carburetion—an idea first introduced to GM's lineup in 1957 both as Oldsmobile's legendary J2 option and under the hoods of Bunkie Knudsen's Pontiacs—was finally made available atop Chevrolet big-blocks in 1967, but only for Corvette customers. Pontiac had been using its famed Tri-Power equipment as the top GTO power option since 1964, then was forced to discontinue the setup (as was Oldsmobile) after 1966 following yet another anti-performance decree from GM's front office, this one banning the use of all multi-carburetor (dual-four and 3x2) induction systems on its divisions' passenger-car engines. The Sting Ray's status as America's only sports car excluded it from this ban, leading to a new big-block Corvette for 1967 that was even more brutal than the previous year's 425hp model.

Chevrolet's 3x2 induction design began with an aluminum intake manifold. Mounted atop that manifold were those three Holleys, with the center two-barrel being the primary fuel-feeder for normal operation. Throttle plates in the two secondary Holley venturis remained closed until revs reached roughly 2000rpm, when a mass-air vacuum signal sent directly from the primary carb's venturi (as opposed to a typical central vacuum

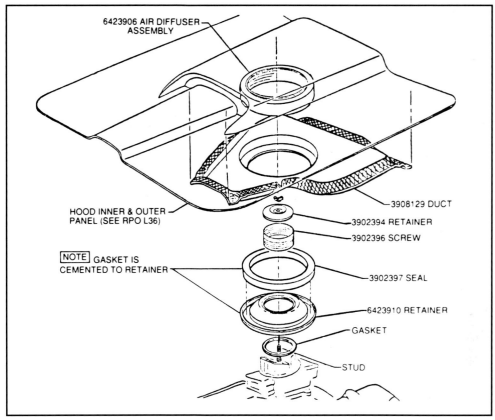

The familiar 1967 big-block hood was for looks only on all models except the L88. The small, open-top air cleaner sealed to the hood's under-side and drew air through a duct running to the back of the scoop where denser air gathered at the windshield's base at high speeds.

source) brought the front and rear two-barrels into the fray in a progression relative to the weight of the driver's foot. By the time engine speeds hit 4000rpm, all three throats were wide open and wailing. Releasing the accelerator activated a mechanical link which positively closed the two secondary throats to avoid instantly overfeeding the engine when it no longer wanted to be fed. Topping everything off was a chrome, triangular, open-element air cleaner.

Benefits of the 3x2 setup involved the best of both worlds. Excellent fuel economy resulted during normal operation as only the humble middle two-barrel was shoveling coal into the fire. But when it came time to fan those flames the other two Holleys quickly entered the fray, almost instantly increasing the system's total flow from roughly 300cfm to a whopping 1,000cfm, making even the biggest four-barrel look like a choker in comparison. Of course, Chevrolet's innovative mass-air 3x2 operation didn't hurt

things, either. As Martyn Schorr wrote, "performance characteristics of [this] three-two setup are unlike those usually associated with a tri-power vehicle. [The] newly developed secondary carburetor control system eliminates the abrupt throttle opening characteristics usually found in most [tri-carb] setups."

After experiencing Chevrolet's tri-carb big-block, *Car and Driver*'s thoroughly impressed writers couldn't resist making comparisons to an earlier innovative Corvette fuel delivery system. "The new system . . . results in an astoundingly tractable engine and uncannily smooth engine response," claimed the magazine's review. "With a venturi area about the size of a barn door, it's possible to drive off in high gear with very little slipping of the clutch or feathering of the throttle. As soon as it's rolling, say at 500rpm, you can push the throttle to the floor and the car just picks up with a turbine-like swelling surge of power that never misses a beat all the way up to its stop speed of

Another marked improvement over previous styling tricks, the distinctive 1967 Corvette's big-block hood may not have been functional but it could certainly turn heads.

over 140mph. On the whole, the Corvette's three deuces are as smooth and responsive as fuel injection."

Chevrolet's "three deuces" were offered in two forms for 1967 Corvettes.

RPO L68 replaced the L36 427's four-barrel with those three Holleys, resulting in a power increase from 390 to 400hp. While most powertrain RPO numbers referred to an engine as a whole, L68 represented the tri-carb setup alone, which was only natural since everything else about the 390 and 400hp 427s was pretty much identical. Window stickers on a 400hp 1967 Corvette showed both RPOs: L36, priced at $200.15, combined with L68,

which tacked on another $105.35, for a total of $305.50. And like the "standard" L36, the 400hp 427 could be backed by the $194.35 Powerglide automatic.

One step beyond was RPO L71, a potent package that almost overnight made the fiberglass faithful forget all about the formidable 425hp L72 of 1966. Everything that had made the L72 so tough—four-bolt mains, a lumpy solid-lifter cam, 11:1 compression, big-valve heads, K66

electronic ignition—was in that package, save, of course, for the big 780cfm Holley four-barrel. With the triple Holleys taking care of fuel-air mixing, the L71 427 produced 435hp at 5800rpm, more than enough muscle to keep Chevrolet's big-block Corvette at the top of Detroit's super-car ranks.

Calling the L71 Sting Ray the "hottest 'Vette yet," Eric Dahlquist explained that it didn't take a powertrain engineer to figure out how the new big-block Corvette stacked up to the competition. Wrote Dahlquist in *Hot Rod*'s May 1967 issue, "ask any kid you meet what the hottest thing going off the showroom floor is and you get one answer: a 435 'Vette." Driving an L71 convertible with the mandatory M21 close-ratio four-speed and standard 3.55:1 Positraction gears, Dahlquist recorded quarter-mile numbers of 13.80sec at 108mph. "GM may not be in racing," he continued, "but its divisions build the best darned line of production

A whole host of safety-conscious features were added inside a Corvette in 1967. Among these were free-wheeling door handles (they were rendered inoperative when the locks were set), four-way flashers, a shatter-resistant day/night mirror, and a "freeway lane change" turn signal system that activated the signal at a touch of the stalk. Also notice the optional headrests, RPO A82, which debuted in 1966.

Right
Three street-legal 427 big-blocks were offered in 1967, this 390hp L36, the 400hp L68, and 435hp top-dog L71. The L36 used a single four-barrel carburetor, while the L68 and L71 were fed by three Holley two-barrels. Basically identical to the L36 save for the triple carbs in place of the single four-barrel, the L68 was priced at $305.50. L68 production was 2,101.

competition cars in the world. The 435 Sting Ray is kind of king of these kings."

Thrashing an identically equipped 1967 convertible, Martyn Schorr bettered

Deuces wild!

Talk about a winning hand! Three deuces to a full-house 427, the Turbo-Jet V8's got it, cold. And that's precisely what Corvette offers, among other things, in the new '67 Sting Ray. In fact, you can order it two ways: 400 horsepower with hydraulic lifters or 435 horses with solid lifters and a real special performance camshaft.

On the other hand, you traditionalists can still get the 427 V8 with a big four-barrel on top, putting out 390 horses. The whole works comes with that well-known Corvette independent rear suspension, 11¾-inch disc brakes all around, new 1967 styling touches and comforts galore. And it has safety features like the GM-developed energy-absorbing steering column and seat belts with pushbutton buckles, standard.

Take the base 300-horsepower Turbo-Fire 327 V8 or order any of the other four engines available. Decide on the extras, like AM-FM radio, you can add. Choose the standard three-speed or Powerglide or the four-speed gearbox you can order. Shuffle up the equipment the way you want it, and deal yourself a Sting Ray.

'67 Corvette

Corvette Sting Ray Sport Coupe with passenger-guard door locks standard for added safety

GM MARK OF EXCELLENCE

CHEVROLET

Chevrolet's triple-carb setup was a mass-air system, meaning it drew vacuum activation for the front and rear Holleys directly from the middle two-barrel's venturi, as opposed to the intake manifold. The effect was a smooth flow of power as all three carburetors began to feed the beast as rpm rose.

Dahlquist's results to the tune of a 12.90sec/111mph time slip and 0–60mph in 5sec flat. In his words, driving an L71 Sting Ray was "sort of like guiding a four-wheeled, two-passenger rocket sled with license plates, an AM-FM radio and stereo tape system!" Concluded Schorr, "the 435-hp Corvette is super-boss, super-quick, super-expensive, [and] super-impossible to insure."

It was also a bit on the super rough side when it came to ride, thanks again to all the weight up front combined with the stiffer springs required to handle that weight. "As such, the 427 model is strictly a smooth-road machine at the posted speed limits," commented Dahlquist. "Granted, once you get wailing, the suspension evens out and sticks to the ground doing it, but there are few places left to run a hundred-twenty for sustained periods." Continued Dahlquist, "the ride is just too severe for any kind of protracted driving, which is a real shame because the Sting Ray's other attributes—steering, balance, adequate leg room, good seat-to-steering-wheel relation, disc brakes that are far superior to anything else we've tried and, of course, the spine-snapping response—are just the right ingredients for a Grand Touring car in anybody's language."

But if Dahlquist thought he'd seen it all, he was wrong. RPO L71 wasn't even the top Corvette option in 1967. RPO L89, priced at $368.65, added a pair of weight-saving aluminum heads to the 435hp L71 427. The idea was nothing new; Duntov had briefly tried optional aluminum cylinder heads atop the 250 and 290hp fuel-injected 283s in 1960, with production attempts reportedly lasting only three months before an unacceptable defect rate forced engineers to revert back to cast-iron fuelie heads. Prospects for a second try at trimming the fat returned once the Mark IV big-block burst on the scene with its extra-heavy load of cast iron.

Adding the L89 heads in 1967 instantly dropped the L71 427's weight by 75lb. Along with their lightweight composition, L89 heads also differed from their L71 counterparts in the combustion chamber area—the L89's intake valves were slightly unshrouded to improve flow—and on the exhaust end, where larger 1.84in valves replaced the standard 1.72in units. No output difference was recorded for the aluminum-head L71, since Duntov's plan was to cut pounds up front, not boost ponies on the road. Did the plan work?

Although only sixteen pairs of L89 cylinder heads were sold in 1967, *Car and Driver* did manage to test a coupe with an aluminum-head L71 427. Explaining that the L89/L71 big-block weighed only 40lb more than the 327 small-block, *Car and Driver*'s editors recorded a front-to-rear weight distribution of 46/54 for their test Corvette, while a typical 327 Sting Ray's distribution was 47/53. Quarter-mile results were listed as 13.6sec at 105mph. By the magazine's account, the L89 option did go a long way toward making a big-block Corvette ride and handle like its small-block brother, basically because those aluminum heads helped put weight distribution back where Duntov knew it belonged.

Of course, overall weight was critical as well, and the Sting Ray had never been as light on its feet as Zora originally had envisioned. After 1963's Grand Sport debacle, it was clear that another lightweight, purpose-built, no-nonsense, high-profile racer would never fly in the face of GM's anti-racing policy. To end-run the anti-performance types, Duntov's engineers kicked off another lightweight Corvette development project in 1965, but this one was based on regular-production options. By essentially "hiding" a collection of race-ready components in Chevrolet parts books, Duntov figured he'd skirt the anti-racing issue. He was right.

Fred Frincke, Cal Wade, and Denny Davis had barely begun work on that parts project when rumors started flying. Writing in *Sports Car Graphic*'s March 1965 issue, Jerry Titus mentioned various performance parts then being planned for the Corvette. "Among the options that will make the car competitive is a new four-speed gearbox designed to handle a 'prodified' [homologated] version of the [Mark IV] engine," claimed Titus. "An estimated 470 horsepower is expected with application of allowable SCCA modifications. We didn't have a chance to test the box. We understand it is quite a bit noisier than the standard Muncie." The "box" Titus referred to was, of course, the M22 Rock Crusher four-speed, officially introduced for 1966. As for the "prodified" engine, that was the fabled L88 427 big-block, easily the greatest Corvette powerplant yet to come down the road. Or racetrack.

From top to bottom, the L88 427 was as "purpose-built" as it got. Although its cylinder block was identical to a typical street-going Mark IV, that certainly was not a detriment considering the standard

high-performance block's four-bolt mains, and terrifically stout lower end. Equally stout was the L88's crankshaft, which was specially forged out of 5140 alloy steel, then cross-drilled for sure lubrication and tuftrided for hardness. Attached to that crank by shot-peened, magnafluxed connecting rods (with heavier 7/16in bolts) were eight forged-aluminum pop-up pistons that squeezed the fuel-air mixture at a molecule-mashing 12.5:1 ratio. Topping things off were the same weight-saving aluminum heads—with their big 2.19in intake and 1.84in exhaust valves—that eventually would be listed under RPO L89.

Feeding the beast was a huge 850cfm Holley four-barrel on a special aluminum intake manifold with its internal partition removed to create an open plenum. Designed by engineer Denny Davis, the L88's solid-lifter cam was radical to say the least, with 337 degrees duration on the intake side, 340 degrees on exhaust, and lift of 0.5365in for the intake valve and 0.5560in for the exhaust. Pushrods were thick 7/16in pieces with hardened ends. On top, special "long-slot" stamped-steel rockers rocked on heat-treated, hardened ball-studs, while

heavy-duty valve springs were held in place by beefed-up retainers and locks. Spark was supplied by the K66 transistorized ignition equipment.

Although a token advertised output of 430hp was bestowed upon the L88 427, to avert any unwanted attention—both from within the corporation and without—actual horsepower was much more than 500. According to engineer Fred Frincke, dyno tests of an L88 with headers produced figures of between 550 and 570hp. Any way you looked at it, the L88 427 was far and away the strongest Corvette powerplant ever produced.

Initial plans called for the L88's release as a 1966 Corvette option. Duntov's engineers had a working example running on a dyno in October 1965, and official 1966 factory paperwork was full of L88 availability references. Chomping at the bit, Jerry Titus couldn't wait to get his hands on an L88 Corvette, and was set to test one late in 1965. The car did not arrive, however, leaving Titus to explain a performance offering he was hoping he wouldn't have to wait much longer to see.

"What was supposed to fill these pages was a track test of an optioned 427, a hundred of which are supposed to

Bob Bondurant and Dick Guldstrand's L88 Corvette leaves the famous starting line at Le Mans in June 1967. Performance early on during the 24 Hours was impressive, with top speeds topping 170mph on the Mulsanne Straight, but a blown engine during the night torpedoed the effort. Dave Friedman photo

be built by January 1 and homologated with both FIA and SCCA," began Titus in December's *Sports Car Graphic.* "Since their retirement from active competition, Chevrolet has been besieged by customers and dealers to at least make hardware available so they could go racing on their own. This program was strictly that, to give the customer something to work with. The package is still in the mill at this writing and *may* see a production line. If rumors are correct, it's nothing too wild; several alloy options—including cylinder heads—that enable you to reduce the

Left
Redline 7.75x15in four-ply nylon tires, RPO QB1, were introduced for 1967 carrying a $46.65 price tag. Sales of RPO QB1 reached 4,230. Total 1967 convertible production, with all engines, was 14,436. New colors included Marina Blue, Lynndale Blue, Elkhart Blue, Goodwood Green, and Marlboro Maroon.

Beneath that distinctive triangular air cleaner are three Holley two-barrels feeding about 1,000cfm into the L71 427. The L71 made 435hp at 5800rpm. Compression was 11:1.

Right
The $42.15 telescopic steering wheel, RPO N36, returned for 1967 with a restyled locking nut/horn button combination. N36 buyers numbered 2,415.

curb weight to around 2600 pounds, and mild engine rework that puts output above 500 horsepower."

Later, in the spring of 1966, *Cars'* Martyn Schorr also made mention of the mysterious new big-block. "Although not listed in the official Chevrolet AMA Sting Ray specifications book," wrote Schorr, "there is another optional 427 which is even more suited for competition. All we know at this time is that this engine does

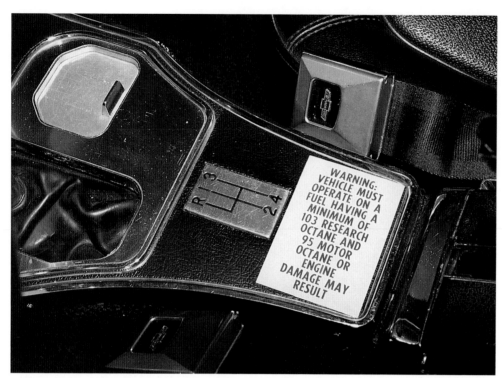

There was little doubt that the L88 was intended only for the track. But those who thought otherwise might have been reminded what they were facing on the street by this warning label on the car's console. Chevrolet press releases made the situation perfectly clear, explaining that "because the L88 is an off-road engine, no provision has been made for anti-pollution control. For those states that require smog-control devices, it cannot be registered for street use in a passenger carrying vehicle."

Another standard feature that helped discourage a driver from taking a 1967 L88 Corvette to the streets (as if the high-strung aluminum-head 427 and brutal Rocker Crusher gearbox weren't convincing enough) was its heavy-duty Harrison aluminum cross-flow radiator, which was installed without a fan shroud—an item race cars rarely need anyway since they almost never end up stuck in traffic. California customers had no choice concerning the car's off-road status since all L88s were delivered with a road draft tube that vented the crankcase directly into the atmosphere, meaning the engines would never meet even the most forgiving emissions standards, let alone the toughest in the country.

As it was, even if a Californian could have driven an L88 legally on the street he would have thought twice about it as soon as he turned the key. The emissions-illegal (in some states like California) L88's 850cfm Holley four-barrel wasn't equipped with a choke—although a retrofit kit was offered by Chevrolet—so starting that hungry, cranky animal was no easy task. Then once running, an L88 427 didn't like to sit calmly as its open-plenum intake, long-duration high-lift cam, and large-port heads completely sacrificed low-speed cooperation for all-out high-rpm performance. Idle speed was a cupboard-rattling 1000rpm. And thanks to that head-cracking 12.5:1 compression, only the next best thing to jet fuel could keep this bomb from pre-detonating. According to delivery paperwork included with an L88, "this unit operates only on Sunoco 260 or equivalent gas of very high octane. Under no circumstances should regular gasoline be used." Those instructions were repeated inside on a label near the shifter: "Warning: vehicle must operate on a fuel having a minimum of 103 research octane and 95 motor octane or engine damage may result." If all that wasn't enough to make everyday operation a drag, L88 Corvettes also couldn't be equipped—no way, no how—with radios. Or power windows. What a bummer.

Completing the L88 lineup was a smaller flywheel, a heavy-duty clutch, and a unique air cleaner. Looking much like no air cleaner at all, the L88 unit featured an open "pan" mounted atop the big Holley carb. In the center of the pan was

exist. Before ordering a Sting Ray for all-out competition it would be wise to check with . . . any dealer who engages in sports or drag competition on the availability of this 'not listed' option."

Duntov had filed L88 homologation papers with both the Sports Car Club of America (SCCA) and the French-run Federation International de L'Automobile (FIA), the governing body for worldwide racing, late in 1965, then quickly delivered a red 1966 427 Corvette coupe, equipped with the L88's big Holley four-barrel and intake, to Roger Penske, who was planning to enter the car in the Daytona 24 Hours race in February 1966. Not even a wreck or a punctured radiator could stop Penske's coupe from finishing first in its class and twelfth overall at Daytona. The car was then repaired, repainted Sunoco Blue, and sent to Sebring, where it was also joined by Penske's Grand Sport roadster, itself now armed with a 427 big-block. Although the Grand Sport would drop out with a blown engine, the coupe

ended up ninth overall for the 12 Hours. It hadn't exactly beaten the world, but Penske's Corvette had proven to Duntov that he definitely needed to get the rest of the L88 parts into production.

Actual release of RPO L88 as an official Corvette option available to the public came in the spring of 1967. Priced at $947.90, the L88 427 was complemented by an impressive list of mandatory heavy-duty pieces. K66 ignition, J56 power-assisted metallic brakes, F41 suspension (which was offered only as an option with the 1967 L71 427), G81 Positraction, and the M22 Rocker Crusher four-speed were all standard equipment along with the L88 427. RPO C48, the heater-defroster delete option offered for Sting Ray buyers since 1963, was included as part of the L88 deal as well since it was relatively easy to assume these cars wouldn't be seeing very much duty away from a racetrack. Deleting the heater/defroster also helped cut loose a few additional pounds.

a small filter; around its edge was a foam gasket. With the hood closed, the gasket sealed the air cleaner to the hood's underside, where ductwork ran back to the rear edge of the Corvette's normally nonfunctional big-block hood scoop. By making this scoop functional, engineers allowed the L88 to take its breaths from the denser air mass that typically gathers at the base of a car's windshield at speed—a clever idea, one that had proven itself under Chevrolet hoods during the Daytona 500 in 1963.

How did the L88 Corvette do on the track? Four aluminum-head 427 Sting Rays went to Sebring in 1967, with the Don Yenko-Dave Morgan car finishing tenth overall and first in class. The 24 Hours of Le Mans in France was the true test, however, and that's where a 1967 L88 coupe showed up that summer with sponsorship from California dealer Dana Chevrolet. With Dick Guldstrand and Bob Bondurant driving, the Dana L88 ran strong in the early going, hitting 171mph on the Mulsanne Straight. But hopes for glory were dashed during the night when a connecting rod exited the side of the block.

Though disappointing, the 1967 Le Mans effort was only the beginning as the L88 kicked off a Corvette racing revival. A second-edition L88 would appear in 1968, followed by a third in 1969. In the hands of Jerry Thompson and Tony De-Lorenzo, the famed Owens-Corning Fiberglass L88 roadsters went on to win eight of eleven SCCA A-Production races in 1968, reviving memories of the glory days before Shelby's Cobras made the scene late in 1962. Production of L88 Corvettes was only twenty in 1967, eighty in 1968, and 116 in 1969.

While Shelby-American's 427 Cobra was still around to taunt Corvette racers on the track in 1967, production of those gnarly monsters had all but ceased that year, leaving Sting Ray drivers on American streets unlimited bragging rights as the baddest boys in the valley. With the

With its "Coke-bottle" body, bulging wheelhouses and pointed nose, the all-new 1968 Corvette followed the first-edition Sting Ray as a proud representative of Chevrolet's long-running legacy of sporty performance and sexy pizzazz.

Chevrolet gave the L88 a token 430hp rating, which was a joke in light of this powerplant's muscular abilities. With a big 850cfm Holley four-barrel, 12.5:1 compression and aluminum heads, the L88 427 easily produced more than 500hp. The K66 transistorized ignition was another mandatory option. Notice the road draft tube equipment exiting the left valve cover. This antiquated setup simply evacuated the crankcase directly into the atmosphere, which is the main reason the L88 was labeled an "off-road" engine.

big-block Cobra gone, the automotive press turned to Shelby's Mustangs as new measuring sticks for this country's only true sports car, and of course the conclusions this time finally favored the Sting Ray hands down. *Motor Trend* squared off a base 300hp 1967 Corvette with a small-block Shelby GT-350 in its April 1967 issue, then followed that with a 435hp Sting Ray big-block versus GT-500 shootout in the May edition. In both cases it was no contest on the road, although *Motor Trend*'s Steve Kelly did

point out that insuring the Shelby Mustangs would be considerably less traumatic than getting coverage for Chevrolet's fiberglass slingshots.

Overall conclusions concerning the last of Chevrolet's first-generation Sting Rays were typically glowing. "The Sting Ray's four-wheel disc brakes are in a class of their own among American cars, and up to the highest standards set abroad," commented *Car and Driver*. They continued, "We have just about exhausted our cherished supply of superlatives for these brakes, so suffice it to say that they're the best." According to *Road & Track*, it was "hard to find fault with the Corvette's handling; it's as near neutral as any car we know and of course there's always enough torque available to steer with the throttle." "All things considered," continued the magazine, "the Sting Ray is a big value for the money. It matches any of its European competition for useful performance and walks away from most of them; it's quiet, luxurious and comfortable under ordinary conditions; easy to

tune and maintain; and even easy on fuel if its performance isn't indulged too often. It remains unique among American cars—and among sports cars."

Chevrolet's 1967 Sting Ray may have been an unintended encore, but what a performance. Five years after the breed first appeared in stunning fashion in the fall of 1962, the last of the so-called midyear Corvettes exited stage right to a standing ovation. Although faster, more modern, better-selling models would follow, they haven't dimmed the first-generation Sting Ray's image in the least. All remain unforgettable.

Right
No readily available external evidence gave away the awesome L88's identity, at least while one was standing still. But with roughly 500 horses beneath that functional hood scoop, there was little doubt that this animal was the wildest Corvette yet. Not street legal in many states in 1967 thanks to its non-existent emissions equipment, this L88 Corvette is one of only twenty built.

Appendix

Corvette Sting Ray Production Figures

1963	coupes	10,594
	convertibles	10,919
	Total	21,513

Other totals:

Standard 250hp 327 V-8	3,892
L75 300hp 327 V-8	8,033
L76 340hp 327 V-8	6,978
L84 360hp 327 F.I. V-8	2,610
Standard three-speed manual transmission	919
M20 Four-speed manual transmission	17,973
M35 Powerglide automatic transmission	2,621
C07 Auxiliary hardtop for convertibles	5,739
C60 Air conditioning	278
G81 Positraction rear axle	17,554

New Sting Rays roll down the St. Louis assembly line in 1963. Notice that the hood vents have been inexplicably airbrushed out on the lead car.

J50 Power brakes	3,336
J65 Sintered-metallic brakes	5,310
N03 36.5gal fuel tank (coupes only)	63
N40 Power steering	3,063
Z06 Special Performance Equipment (coupes only)	199

1964	coupes	8,304
	convertibles	13,925
	Total	22,229

Other totals:

Standard 250hp 327 V-8	3,262
L75 300hp 327 V-8	10,471
L76 365hp 327 V-8	7,171
L84 375hp 327 F.I. V-8	1,325
Standard three-speed manual transmission	715
M20 Four-speed manual transmission	19,034
M35 Powerglide automatic transmission	2,480
C07 Auxiliary hardtop for convertibles	7,023
C60 Air conditioning	1,988
F40 Special suspension	82
G81 Positraction rear axle	18,279
J50 Power brakes	2,270
J56 Special sintered-metallic brakes	29
J65 Sintered-metallic brakes, power-assisted	4,780
K66 Transistorized ignition	552
N03 36.5gal fuel tank (coupes only)	38
N11 Off-road exhaust system	1,953
N40 Power steering	3,126
P48 Cast-aluminum knock-off wheels	806

1965	coupes	8,186
	convertibles	15,376
	Total	23,562

Other totals:

Standard 250hp 327 V-8	2,549
L75 300hp 327 V-8	8,358
L76 365hp 327 V-8	5,011
L78 425hp 396 V-8	2,157
L79 350hp 327 V-8	4,716
L84 375hp 327 F.I. V-8	771
Standard three-speed manual transmission	434
M20 Four-speed manual transmission	21,107
M35 Powerglide automatic transmission	2,021
C07 Auxiliary hardtop for convertibles	7,787
C60 Air conditioning	2,423
F40 Special suspension	975
G81 Positraction rear axle	19,965
J50 Power brakes	4,044
J61 Drum brake substitution credit	316
K66 Transistorized ignition	3,686
N03 36.5-gallon fuel tank (coupes only)	41
N11 Off-road exhaust system	2,468
N14 Sidemount exhausts	759
N32 Teakwood steering wheel	2,259
N36 Telescopic steering column	3,917
N40 Power steering	3,236
P48 Cast-aluminum knock-off wheels	1,116

1966	coupes	9,958
	convertibles	17,762
	Total	27,720

Other totals:

Standard 300hp 327 V-8	9,755
L36 390hp 427 V-8	5,116
L72 425hp 427 V-8	5,258
L79 350hp 327 V-8	7,591
Standard three-speed manual transmission	564
M20 Four-speed manual transmission (wide-ratio)	10,837
M21 Four-speed manual transmission (close-ratio)	13,903
M22 Heavy-duty four-speed manual trans. (close-ratio)	15
M35 Powerglide automatic transmission	2,401
C07 Auxiliary hardtop for convertibles	8,463
C60 Air conditioning	3,520
F41 Special suspension	2,705
G81 Positraction rear axle	24,056
J50 Power brakes	5,464
J56 Special heavy-duty brakes	382
K66 Transistorized ignition	7,146
N03 36.5gal fuel tank (coupes only)	66
N11 Off-road exhaust system	2,795
N14 Sidemount exhausts	3,617
N32 Teakwood steering wheel	3,941
N36 Telescopic steering column	3,670
N40 Power steering	5,611
P48 Cast-aluminum knock-off wheels	1,194

1967	coupes	8,504
	convertibles	14,436
	Total	22,940

Other totals:

Standard 300hp 327 V-8	6,858
L36 390hp 427 V-8	3,832
L68 400hp 427 V-8	2,101
L71 435hp 427 V-8	3,754
L79 350hp 327 V-8	6,375
L88 430hp 427 V-8 (with aluminum cylinder heads)	20
L89 Aluminum cylinder heads for L71 427	16
Standard three-speed manual transmission	424
M20 Four-speed manual transmission (wide-ratio)	9,157
M21 Four-speed manual transmission (close-ratio)	11,015
M22 Heavy-duty four-speed manual trans. (close-ratio)	20
M35 Powerglide automatic transmission	2,324
C07 Auxiliary hardtop for convertibles	6,880
C60 Air conditioning	3,788
F41 Special suspension	2,198
G81 Positraction rear axle	20,308
J50 Power brakes	4,766
J56 Special heavy-duty brakes	267
K19 Air injection reactor	2,573
K66 Transistorized ignition	5,759
N03 36.5-gallon fuel tank (coupes only)	2
N14 Sidemount exhausts	4,209
N36 Telescopic steering column	2,415
N40 Power steering	5,747
N89 Cast-aluminum wheels	720

Chevrolet's 1965 Corvette convertible with small-block power

Corvette Engine Specifications

	RPO	CID	Horsepower	Torque	Induction	Comp.
1963	Std.	327	250 @ 4400rpm	350 @ 2800rpm	Carter 4-bbl.	10.5:1
	L75	327	300 @ 5000rpm	360 @ 3200rpm	Carter AFB 4-bbl.	10.5:1
	L76	327	340 @ 6000rpm	344 @ 4000rpm	Carter AFB 4-bbl.	11.25:1
	L84	327	360 @ 6000rpm	352 @ 4000rpm	Rochester fuel-inj.	11.25:1

NOTE: Base engine and L75 327 had hydraulic lifters; L76 and L84 high-performance 327s had solid lifters.

	RPO	CID	Horsepower	Torque	Induction	Comp.
1964	Std.	327	250 @ 4400rpm	350 @ 2800rpm	Carter 4-bbl.	10.5:1
	L75	327	300 @ 5000rpm	360 @ 3200rpm	Carter AFB 4-bbl.	10.5:1
	L76	327	365 @ 6200rpm	350 @ 4000rpm	Holley 4-bbl.	11:1
	L84	327	375 @ 6200rpm	350 @ 4400rpm	Rochester fuel-inj.	11:1

NOTE: Base engine and L75 327 had hydraulic lifters; L76 and L84 high-performance 327s had solid lifters.

	RPO	CID	Horsepower	Torque	Induction	Comp.
1965	Std.	327	250 @ 4400rpm	350 @ 2800rpm	Carter 4-bbl.	10.5:1
	L75	327	300 @ 5000rpm	360 @ 3200rpm	Carter AFB 4-bbl.	10.5:1
	L76	327	365 @ 6200rpm	350 @ 4000rpm	Holley 4-bbl.	11:1
	L78	396	425 @ 6400rpm	415 @ 4000rpm	Holley 4-bbl.	11:1
	L79	327	350 @ 5800rpm	360 @ 3600rpm	Holley 4-bbl.	11:1
	L84	327	375 @ 6200rpm	350 @ 4400rpm	Rochester fuel-inj.	11:1

NOTE: Base engine, L75 and L79 327s all had hydraulic lifters; L76 and L84 327s had solid lifters, as did the 425hp 396 big-block V-8.

	RPO	CID	Horsepower	Torque	Induction	Comp.
1966	Std.	327	300 @ 5000rpm	360 @ 3400rpm	Holley 4-bbl.	10.25:1
	L36	427	390 @ 5200rpm[1]	460 @ 3600rpm	Holley 4-bbl.	10.25:1
	L72	427	425 @ 5600rpm[2]	460 @ 4000rpm	Holley 4-bbl.	11:1
	L79	327	350 @ 5800rpm	360 @ 3600rpm	Holley 4-bbl.	11:1

[1] L36 was briefly advertised at 400 hp early in production
[2] L72 was briefly advertised at 450 hp early in production
NOTE: Base engine, L79 327 and L36 427 all had hydraulic lifters; the 425hp L72 427 had solid lifters. The L36 390hp 427 also had two-bolt mainbearing caps, while the L72 big-block had four-bolt mains.

	RPO	CID	Horsepower	Torque	Induction	Comp.
1967	Std.	327	300 @ 5000rpm	360 @ 3400rpm	Holley 4-bbl.	10.25:1
	L36	427	390 @ 5400rpm	460 @ 3600rpm	Holley 4-bbl.	10.25:1
	L68[1]	427	400 @ 5400rpm	460 @ 3600rpm	3 Holley 2-bbls.	10.25:1
	L71	427	435 @ 5800rpm	460 @ 4000rpm	3 Holley 2-bbls.	11:1
	L79	327	350 @ 5800rpm	360 @ 3600rpm	Holley 4-bbl.	11:1
	L88[2]	427	430 @ 5200rpm	450 @ 4400rpm	Holley 4-bbl.	12.5:1
	L89[3]	427	435 @ 5800rpm	460 @ 4000rpm	3 Holley 2-bbls.	11:1

[1] L68 option added the 3x2 Holley carburetor setup atop the L36 427 in place of the 390hp 427's single Holley four-barrel, upping the advertised output to 400 hp.
[2] L88 option featured special race-only 427 with aluminum heads and no provisions for street-legal emissions controls. Advertised horsepower and torque figures shown here were token numbers—actual output was much higher, easily surpassing 500 horsepower.
[3] L89 option simply added aluminum heads to the L71 435hp 427 resulting in no changes for advertised output.
NOTE: Base engine, L79 327, L36 427, and L68 427 all had hydraulic lifters; the 425hp L71 427 and L88 special-performance 427 had solid lifters. The L36 390hp and L68 400hp 427s also had two-bolt main bearing caps, while the L71 and L88 big-blocks had four-bolt mains.

Right
Chevrolet's 1965 396ci Mk IV big-block shows off its "porcupine" canted-valve heads.

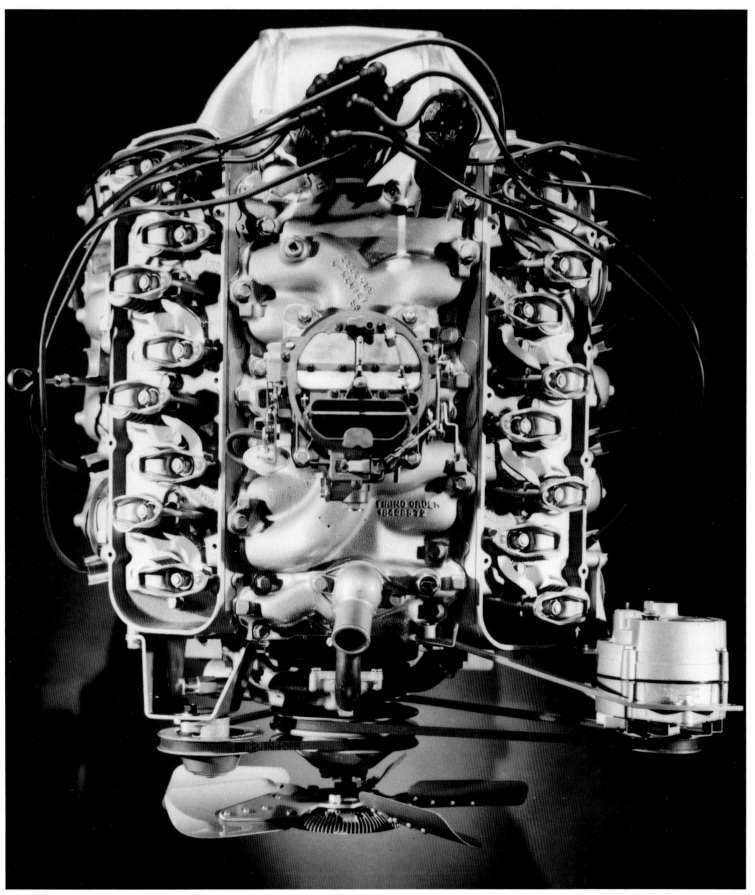

Index